Charles Seale-Hayne Library

University of Plymouth

(01752) 588 588

LibraryandITenquiries@plymouth.ac.uk

101 — activity — Appendice
        to &of the
            class

10 —

43 —

148. —

BASIC BOOKS IN EDUCATION

Editor: *Kathleen O'Connor, B.Sc., Senior Lecturer in Education, Rolle College, Exmouth*
Advisory Editor: *D. J. O'Connor, M.A., Ph.D., Professor of Philosophy, University of Exeter*

Creativity and the Teacher

The implication of 'the ability explosion' is that teachers should be able to cater for, develop, and extend a wide range, or veritable explosion, of abilities. This book deals essentially with the practical issues encountered. It discusses the problems involved in encouraging creative response and personal responsibility in pupils and introduces many original ideas on creativity: ideas for assessment and rating of creative abilities in mathematics, creative writing, physical education, art, model-making, and drama; questionnaires for the assessment of creative potential through the use of self, peer and teacher ratings. It also covers some of the more popular verbal and non-verbal creativity tests. The book is based on a research inquiry carried out with a group of middle school pupils.

There are summaries and 'further reading' lists at the end of each chapter, and there is a full bibliography, glossary and index.

Creativity and the Teacher

JOHN FOSTER, M.Ed.
DEPUTY PRINCIPAL LADY MABEL COLLEGE OF EDUCATION
WENTWORTH WOODHOUSE
ROTHERHAM, YORKS

MACMILLAN

First published 1971
Published by
MACMILLAN EDUCATION LTD
Basingstoke and London
Companies and representatives
throughout the world

Printed in Great Britain by
ROBERT MACLEHOSE AND CO LTD
The University Press, Glasgow

0 - 3 3 3 - 1 1 6 28 - 3

0 1 0 8 8 4 1

Contents

Acknowledgements

I would like to acknowledge the help I have received from various sources in preparing this manuscript. I am grateful to Messrs Holt, Reinhart and Winston for permission to use material from 'Modes of thinking in young children' by M. A. Wallach and N. Kogan. My thanks are also due to Professor Paul Torrance of the University of Georgia for permission to use extracts from his tests, and to Professor Kaoru Yamamoto of Pennsylvania State University who allowed me to use parts of his scoring procedures.

I am especially grateful to Professor J. E. Nesbitt, of the New University of Ulster, for his help with the research from which this book emanates, and to the head-teachers, staffs and children in the schools used in my inquiries. Students at Manchester College of Education assisted me enormously in the assessment of scripts used in the research, and I am deeply indebted to innumerable other colleagues who have been a great source of help and encouragement.

John Foster
Lady Mabel College of Education
Wentworth Woodhouse
Rotherham, Yorks

Introduction

There will be a few teachers who are not familiar with the word 'creativity'. Over the last twenty years it has been used to indicate possible cures for all the ills which bedevil the education system. It has become a very emotive term; a campaigning banner for some and anathema to others. Yet throughout all the academic discussion teachers have seen that the ideas emanating from a study of creative functioning have a fundamental relevance to their work. This book is an attempt to refine and interpret some of the main issues, and relate them directly to the work of the teacher. The approach will not be technical, but more reflective and evaluative.

It is not the aim of this book to make a comprehensive survey of the whole field of creativity. For this, the reader is referred to the short reading list at the end of this introduction. Rather, the aim here is to highlight certain aspects which have great interest for teachers, and illustrate these with original material. The background material included has been selected in order to give the reader the necessary basis for a full understanding of the ideas which are introduced.

Many schools are now adopting more progressive and often informal approaches to learning, which stress discovery techniques and inductive methods of teaching. As this trend progresses, new philosophies emerge. The re-thinking involved takes more account of the child as an active agent in his own learning. It emphasises the importance of the individual's involvement in what he is doing, and sees one of the basic needs of children as a desire for some kind of expression. This approach values individual creative response, and so places creativity at the core of the school's planning for its children. It becomes central to all the preparation for learning and the nexus of the total educative process.

Material used in this book has been collected from many sources, including research projects and normal classroom activities. Much of it is based on an individual study which I have undertaken recently. An outline of this work is given in Appendix 1. When formulating my research, I was struck by the fact that little specific study had been concerned with creativity in English junior schools. By far the greater part of the work had been American, and a substantial portion of this had been studying adults and older children.

In view of the different child-rearing practices and school systems existing in America, it is not always either accurate or desirable to generalise from this work to situations involving English children in English schools.

I decided to undertake this study as an exploratory inquiry concerning creativity in English children during the middle years of schooling.

The few English studies which have been undertaken have usually been concerned with a specific problem, such as the reliability of a test, the effect of restriction of ability range in a sample, or the replication of a design originally studied elsewhere. This seemed to indicate the need for an investigation covering all aspects of the creative work and thinking of children in English schools.

For my research I accepted the view of Guilford (40) that 'Creativity is not a special gift of the select few. It is, instead, a property shared by all humanity, to a greater or smaller degree.' I thought this had great educational importance, and indeed both Torrance (93) and MacKinnon (in 78) have shown that in individual pragmatic practice educators resent the creative, the bold and the unusual student. However, the knowledge of the nature of creativity, the creative personality, the identification of creative talent, the creative process, and the environment conducive to creative activity is still very tentative. My study represents an individual exploratory attempt to present a wide range of data from a group of children which may indicate some refinement of our understanding of this very relevant problem of today.

A BASIC READING LIST IN CREATIVITY

Cropley, A. J. *Creativity* (Longman 1967)

Freeman, J., Butcher, T. and Christie, H. J. *Creativity. A Selective Review of Research* (Society for Research in Higher Education 1968)

Getzels, J. W. and Jackson, P. W. *Creativity and Intelligence* (John Wiley & Sons 1962)

Hudson, L. *Contrary Imaginations* (Methuen 1966)

Koestler, A. *The Act of Creation* (Hutchinson 1964)

Shields, J. B. *The Gifted Child* (National Foundation for Educational Research 1968)

Torrance, E. P. *Guiding Creative Talent* (Prentice Hall 1962)

Wallach, M. A. and Kogan, N. *Modes of Thinking in Young Children* (Holt, Reinhart & Winston 1965)

1 The Psychological Bases of Creativity

In this chapter ideas regarding the nature of creativity, its relationship to intelligence and achievement, the measurement of creativity, characteristics of the creative personality and various attempts to evaluate creative behaviour will be discussed and used as an introduction to the study of the topic, giving the reader the background of theoretical knowledge which is necessary in order to understand more specific work introduced later.

WHAT IS CREATIVITY?

Attempts to define creativity are found throughout the literature. This elusive area of human functioning has been a study for psychologists and philosophers throughout the centuries, and attempts to define it are so diverse as to present a meaningless picture if they are viewed in isolation from the thoughts and situations which engendered them. They range from the psychological to the philosophical, from the sociological to the statistical, from total specificity to complete generality. Definitions can be classified under many different headings, and in looking at research work it is important for teachers to know how the investigator has defined creativity in order to assess the usefulness of the results. It is also very important to know what CRITERIA have been used in the evaluation of creative endeavours. The criterion problem is central to the study of creativity and is largely unresolved. Probably it needs to be discussed by teachers against the actual background of their own work and the children they are teaching at the time. These discussions may centre around the following points:

1 Did the creative act give any satisfaction to the child concerned?

2 How did other children react to the creative pursuit being considered?

3 Was something produced which was new to the child?

4 Was the idea the child's own or was it the response to some stimulus provided by someone else?

5 Were the limits of the child's potential stretched during the work?

6 How can teachers tell whether creative thinking has taken place?

7 By what standards will creative products be judged?

8 Are certain personality qualities associated with creative performance?

9 What kind of classroom environment stimulates creative behaviour?

10 What kind of teacher attitude and pupil/teacher relationship encourage creativity?

DEFINITIONS OF CREATIVITY USEFUL TO THE PRACTISING TEACHER

Schachtel (83) looks at the basic motivation behind the individual's quest for creative experience. He sees this as being concerned with 'the openness of the individual to the world around him'. This is the ability to remain receptive to the experiences provided by the environment and to see, continually, the possibilities for further development. Children in school are put in the position of responding creatively, in these terms, every time a teacher presents a stimulus for their consideration, comment, and as a basis for their own work.

The work of Koestler (55), although subjective and voicing a personal opinion, is nevertheless based on the study of a wide range of creative personalities, their modes of thought and their creative products. He sees creativity as involving 'bisociation'; the ability to draw together unusual frames of reference. When this is done, Koestler claims, the result may be laughter, tears or, at the highest level, creation. Most tests of creativity (see Chapter 4) ask children to draw together unusual frames of reference, For example, 'Tell me all the ways in which a radio and a telephone are alike'. In school teachers ask children to do this in hundreds of ways. For example, when they say things like 'What else would stick it better?' or 'Is there anything in the waste-box which you can adapt to make a chimney for the model?' or 'Does the work you have done in geography on monsoon rains help you to describe more vividly the floods we have experienced here?' The bisociation theme of Koestler's is a central, omnibus idea, similar in spirit to that proposed by Ghiselin (33), who suggests that creativity is 'the process of change, of development, of evolution in the organisation of subjective life'. These ideas are really pointers towards more specific definitions which have an even more direct bearing on the work of the teacher. Parker (73) describes creativity as 'the art of seeking out, trying out and combining knowledge in new ways'. He stresses the value to the individual of the production of something new to the individual performing the act. Parker's view is used considerably in the work described in Chapter 3 to assess a wild range of creative abilities forming part of the normal school curriculum. Teachers often demand creative thought in Parker's terms when they ask children to make judgements and solve complex problems. John and Michael, aged 12 years, were asked to invent a new alphabet and translate a letter into this when they were finding out about techniques of encoding and decoding. Here they had a body of knowledge, but were asked to use it afresh by presenting it in new ways.

Kneller (54) says that 'Creative thought is innovative, exploratory, venturesome, impatient of convention, attracted to the unknown and undetermined'. In other words, it contains the elements of Guilford's (38) DIVERGENT THINKING and Wertheimer's (109) PRODUCTIVE THOUGHT. The ability to think creatively, in these terms, is again required by teachers in most informal learning experiences.

Both Haefele (43) and Mednick (70) have stressed that creativity involves the ability to make new combinations but they also lay emphasis on the social worth of the new combinations, thus precluding unusual answers which are purely bizarre. To develop Haefele's ideas, he says that creativity is the ability to make new combinations; the creative process is the means of making them; the new combination is an innovation, and high creativity is the ability to make innovations of social worth. It is rewarding for teachers to analyse, in these terms, some of the work they plan for children, and to see how easily their preparation fits into this definition. Many teachers would question Haefele's concept of 'social worth', and point out that a child may be highly creative in producing a realistic innovation even if it appeared to have no social worth. I don't see these two viewpoints as being in opposition to each other. Haefele is particularly concerned with the evaluation of creative endeavours according to objective standards, while the teachers' view expressed is more concerned with creativity as the essence of self, as a means of individual expression. Creative thinking, in both these terms, is likely to include the elements of both REALITY–ADJUSTED, and AUTISTIC THINKING. Reference to McKellar's work in the Further Reading section at the end of this chapter would develop this theme for the interested reader.

Barron (5) sees the creative personality as having 'a disposition towards originality'. Teachers may well ask themselves whether this definition characterises creative children in their class or just 'the awkward squad'. Or maybe the latter are unrecognised members of the former group!

Creativity is probably best viewed by the teacher as a very complex dimension covering all aspect of behaviour, and will include all the abilities involved in reinterpreting ideas induced by a variety of stimuli, as well as the abilities required in innovating new ideas.

CREATIVITY AND ITS RELATIONSHIP TO INTELLECT AND ACHIEVEMENT

Torrance (93), in a survey of recent literature in the area of creative thinking, claims that, although sporadic reports can be found on the topic dated as early as the nineteenth century, systematic research emanated from Guilford's address to the

American Psychological Association in 1950 when he called their attention to lack of research in this area. However, in order to understand recent research better it is relevant to identify some of the earlier work and show its influence. Burt (10) has traced the main landmarks clearly and shown their relevance to current thought in the psychology of creative ability. The main landmarks he proposes are Galton's work for the systematic testing of 'higher mental processes' and the attempts of Galton's students and associates to construct practicable tests of 'productive thinking'. Even in the first decade of this century, Galton isolated 'special aptitudes' of fluency ('an unusual and spontaneous flow of images and ideas'), receptivity and intuition or insight, as being components of the creative process. McDougall, following Galton's lead, added to this list productive or deviant association, and all workers in this school recognised the importance of an ambiguous quality referred to as 'zeal'. The contribution of this early work can be seen not only as delineating specific areas for later inquiry, but also in establishing terminology which is still used today for communication of ideas in this area of study.

Workers in the previous century and the early years of this used a variety of statistical techniques to help them in their research. The work of Galton and Pearson in the nineteenth century had provided an index called the CORRELATION COEFFICIENT for expressing the correspondence between any two sets of measurements for a group of people. Readers wishing to follow up this concept should refer to Dr King's book in the Further Reading section of this chapter. It was after the First World War, however, that Kelley at Harvard, Thurstone at Chicago and others in America and England began to use a sophisticated mathematical technique called 'factor analysis' to help them analyse their results. This technique has developed greatly since those early days, especially so since the advent of computers. It now forms the basis of the work of most psychologists studying the structure of human abilities, especially the Guilford school, whose work will be discussed later. Factor analysis is too complicated to describe mathematically; for this the reader should consult Fruchter's book (details in the Further Reading section). A very simple, naïve analogy would be that it is like putting all the test results in a tub and stirring them up. This action brings together into lumps those variables which have something in common. These lumps are the factors which can be taken out and named. The purpose of factor analysis is to enable the researcher to account for the test results with the fewest number of independent variables. There are usually several factors present in any psychological test, and the interpretation of factor analysis can involve fundamental disagreements among psychologists. A knowledge of the use made of this technique will help the reader to appreciate more fully the development of work in this field.

One particular investigation which made an important contribution to later work in the area was that of Garnett (31). He devised further tests on the lines developed by Galton and suggested the existence of a 'c' factor which represented 'cleverness'. This was concerned with quickness of apprehension, verbal humour and the ability to produce unique responses. In effect, Garnett saw cleverness as associated with wit and originality. He thought it occurred in people who could think using complex thought structures, and who could associate unusual ideas freely with ease and fluency. He deduced that subjects having a high rating on this 'c' factor would be able to break away from accepted ways of solving problems and reach solutions by more imaginative and devious routes. Although there is a certain naïvety in Garnett's rather pedantic pronouncement on the structure of this ability, there do seem to be links between his ideas and both the PSYCHOMETRIC approach of Guilford and the 'bisociation' theory of Koestler. Garnett's study was heavily criticised by Kelley (53) because it was based on personal judgements and not objective test scores. Kelley concluded 'that our final belief in deviousness as a factor must be most uncertain', basing this opinion on the impossibility of the experiment being replicated.

Hargreaves (44) called attention to the role of imagination in creative thinking, and contributed the idea of an 'f' factor. This constituted a 'fluency' factor, which he claimed represented the essential element in imagination. Burt (11) suggests this is a similar element to that identified by him earlier as 'productive imagination' or 'inventiveness' and also to the characteristic described by

Galton as 'fluency'. McKellar (68) collates a great deal of experimental study in the fields of imagination and thinking, and attempts to show the link between imagination and original, creative thinking. He also illustrates the interactions of autistic and reality-adjusted thinking in the creative process.

Spearman summed up his own views on creative ability in a book called *The Creative Mind*, published in 1930. He believed that a factor of general ability (g) was involved in all creative activities, and he did not think that any single factor of creative ability existed as an entity. His view was that imagination, in the sense of creativeness or originality, depended solely on what we call 'intelligence'. Throughout the years many investigators have taken issue with this view, but recent work by Hildreth (47) and Marsh (63) has lent support once more to some of Spearman's ideas. In particular the evidence they present against the existence of a separate factor of creativity is in line with the early views expressed by Spearman.

One approach which has been tried by researchers to discover something of the relationship of creativity to intellect and achievement has involved analysing in detail the personality of recognised 'high creatives', the process by which they work, what they have produced and the environment which stimulates them. This is a rather intuitive, subjective method, but Ghiselin (33) has shown that it can be fruitful in indicating common features of the creative personality, insight into the creative process, and the individual cues from the environment which seem to be necessary for creative acts to take place in some people. Inference is made regarding the relationship of creativity to intellect and achievement, but the results are inconclusive and certainly would not stand up to rigorous scientific scrutiny.

Mention has been made of Guilford's now-famous 1950 Presidential Address. This marked a revival of American interest in creativity and heralded a new era of work in this field led by Guilford and his associates at the University of Southern California. Guilford (38) believes in a very wide view of what we call 'intelligence'. His total picture of 'intelligence' includes a variety of creative abilities. In his view there are many factors of intellect which are undiscovered because we lack the means to measure them, and unstimulated because the education system fails to elicit them. His picture of intelligence is presented in chart form and is called 'The structure of intellect'. It is a theoretical model and postulates 120 possible factors to make up his structural view of intelligence. Although this model is extremely theoretical, it does show how factor analysis can progressively isolate more and more components of intelligence. From this work has emerged the idea that there are PRIMARY TRAITS OF CREATIVITY. These are concerned with fluency and originality of response, flexibility of thinking, and the ability to invent new ideas and elaborate on simple ones. Anastasi (1), commenting on the work of Guilford and his associates, presents a balanced view of this concept of creativity in concluding:

Although tests of the above factors probably come closest to measuring the essential psychological aspects of creativity, many other abilities are undoubtedly needed for effective creative achievement. Many cognitive, evaluative and divergent aptitudes usually classified under reasoning are needed but these are probably measured in intelligence tests as they exist at present.

This view will be easily accepted by teachers who readily see verbal reasoning ability, and a variety of creative abilities going hand in hand in general classroom problem-solving activities.

The literature dealing with the nature of creativity and its relationship to intellect and achievement can be broadly divided into two groups:

1   Those who propose that creativity is a distinct aspect of intellectual functioning which is, for all practical purposes, independent of conventional intelligence.

2   Those who submit that creativity is dependent upon unique cognitive factors which function within the hierarchial structure of intelligence proposed by Vernon (99).

This distinction is also largely unresolved, but it is useful to examine these two opposing viewpoints.

The first standpoint is taken by Getzels and Jackson (32), who focused attention on the relationship of creative abilities to academic achievement when they selected two groups of children which they called 'High I.Q.' and 'High Creative' respectively. The first group contained children who were in the top 20 per cent on I.Q., but not on creativity. In the second group were those children who were in the top 20 per cent on creativity, but not on I.Q. The average I.Q. of the high I.Q. group was twenty-three points above that of the high creatives, but in spite of this there were no significant differences in academic achievement between the two. Consequently, it was implied that creativity can compensate in some way for relative lack of skill in the areas sampled by more conventional intelligence tests. Perhaps the most significant conclusion from the Getzels and Jackson study, in this context, was that they inferred that while creativity is slightly related to intelligence, it really constitutes a separate cognitive factor which owes little to conventional intelligence. It must be remembered, however, that in Getzels and Jackson's sample, the high creative group, which was selected in such a way as to exclude students of really high I.Q., still had an average I.Q. of 127. It has been suggested that selecting the sample in this way was a prime factor in producing the results they obtained. This work is important, though, as it has led to what is called 'the threshold theory', which asserts that beyond a certain I.Q. (the suggested cut-off is 120) there is little or no relationship between intelligence and creativity, and that being more 'intelligent' is no guarantee of a corresponding increase in creativity. When a similar technique is used with the complete ability range, it is more difficult to find support for the independence of creativity from intelligence, as will be seen. Torrance (94) replicated the Getzels and Jackson study at junior-school level in America on several occasions, and he did report similar findings. He said that in his sample there was only a 30 per cent overlap between the top fifth in intelligence (as measured by a conventional I.Q. test) and the top fifth in creativity (as rated by class-mates and teachers). This lent some support to the idea of the independence of the intelligence and creativity variables. Here again it must be remembered that highly selective groups, covering a small ability range, were used, and this could have been a significant factor in producing these results.

Some of the issues raised by the Getzels and Jackson work

were tested experimentally by Ripple and May (78) and Yamamoto (116). Their results did not support the view that 'creativity is an entity independent of other facets of human intellect'. Sultan (86) reports a factorial study in this field. He tried to isolate the primary traits of creative thinking proposed by Guilford and resolve them into more familiar factors, such as 'g' and verbal and spatial abilities. Guilford's creativity factors were not readily measurable in Sultan's sample of 13–14-year-old grammar-school pupils, but were resolved into 'g', 'v' and 'k', together with a fluency factor. These findings are not at variance with some of Guilford's data. He does show (in Anderson (2)) that creativity involves essentially the capacity to invent and innovate, whereas conventional intelligence requires rather the reproduction of the already learned. In these terms, Guilford sees creativity as part of his structure of intellect model and concludes: 'Thus it appears that each primary, intellectual ability represents a kind of cross-road or intersection of a certain kind of operation, applied to a certain kind of material yielding to a certain kind of product.' The two pieces of work by Sultan and Guilford illustrate the complexity of creativity and the possibility of subdividing it in many different ways. Vernon (101) comments on this and notes the overlapping of the factors as outlined by both Sultan and Guilford. Teachers must view these researches carefully and assess them against their classroom experiences in order to help to elucidate a clearer interpretation. Is intelligence the multi-dimensional concept, components of which it is possible to isolate by factor analysis, and are components of creative ability also components of intelligence? This is a fundamental question which teachers must consider.

Lait (56), studying the relationship of various school factors to creativity, supports the Getzels and Jackson study, but Hasan and Butcher (46) find their results not generally applicable. Replicating the study with Scottish children, they summarised that

It might be possible to distinguish by means of open-ended tests of divergent thinking a set of able children whose abilities have hitherto been concealed or minimised by the use of conventional tests. Our results seem to indicate that this will not easily be possible in an unselected group of children by means of the open-ended tests at present available.

A similar mixed reception for the Getzels and Jackson findings is reported by Edwards and Tyler (25). In fact, the Getzels and Jackson study has been widely criticised, particularly in England, on both methodological and statistical grounds. Foremost amongst the critics have been Burt (11) and Marsh (63), who concludes that

the arguments advanced [by him] and the details analysed of the author's correlations would seem to indicate that creativity is determined by different phenomena than Getzels and Jackson assume. Rather than being almost independent of the general factor of intelligence, this factor is the most constant and conspicuous ingredient. The conventional I.Q. is still the best single criterion for creative potential. This may be improved upon by the use of other tests as well.

Hudson (49), working in England with upper forms in grammar schools, delineates two types of clever schoolboys, the CONVERGER and the DIVERGER, which he tentatively links with high I.Q. and high creative performance respectively. It is Hudson's description of the intellectual and personal differences between these two which are useful to teachers, and which may help them to cater more effectively for the differing personalities who make up their classes. His ideas on what makes pupils opt for science or arts courses are also pertinent to the work of teachers, and may help them in counselling and guidance work.

Many tests of creativity are concerned with providing unusual associations and relationships. These are based on Mednick's (70) concept of creativity, where he defines the creative process as 'the forming of associative elements into new combinations which either meet specified requirements or are in some way useful'. Wallach and Kogan (106) used this approach and appeared to isolate an aspect of thinking which stood apart from the traditional concept of general intelligence.

One of the major contributions they have made is in the critical analysis of the concept of the 'test' of creativity, the very idea of which seems to them to be anathema to creative pursuits. Their rationale stressed informality, relaxed conditions, no time-limits and a game-like approach.

Other studies that have provided evidence of creativity as a separate dimension of intellectual functioning are Anderson (3), Cropley (16, 17), Thorndike (91) and Yamamoto (113). These reports all indicate that creativity may be viewed as a separate entity from intelligence, but suggest that there may be differing numbers of factors of creativity and not one unitary trait. Cropley (17) found ultimately

that high scores on tests of divergent thinking will tend to be accompanied by high scores on tests of convergent thinking, and vice-versa, although the two kinds of thinking are not identical, and it supports the suggestion that conventional skills may provide the basis upon which creative productions rest as Bruner (9) and Pribram (74) have suggested.

This statement certainly seems to reflect the intuitive thoughts of most experienced teachers on this subject. It is, however, a productive view in so far as it may lead teachers to search out children who have abilities not tested by more traditional forms of intelligence testing.

The second group of studies in this section, supporting the hypothesis that creativity results largely from the operation of 'general ability' contains both original work and critical appraisals of other studies. In the latter category, Burt (11), in a critical review of Getzels and Jackson's work, asserts that British investigators seem agreed 'that in all of them [creative activities], general intelligence is an essential and indeed the most important ingredient'. Support is lent to this position by Wall (105), who was specifically concerned with the education of the gifted. He postulates that creativity is likely to result from a well-stored mind and that relatively high intelligence is necessary for this as well as a certain fineness of perception. Certainly my own study provides further support for Wall's first point, in that children rated highly in creative pursuits were children with an intrinsic interest in the activity who had a wide background of experience from which to make creative generalisations. Several American sources also produce evidence in favour of this viewpoint – namely, McNemar (69), Gardner (30) and Wallen (107), who decries the tendency to over-generalise findings, to imply that creativity and intelligence are different and to forget the lack of RELIABILITY and VALIDITY in present creativity tests. Wodtke (111), studying reliability and validity problems, also failed to find support in his data for the view that creativity and intelligence tests are unrelated. He saw no evidence of the independence of creativity and intelligence and no evidence that intelligence measures do not contribute substantially to such predictions in unselected groups.

Looking at the classification of abilities, Vernon (100) regards intelligence as a fluid collection of infinitely varied thinking abilities, and quarrels with Guilford's structure of intellect model, which he thinks carries to extreme the breaking down of intelligence into different components. He concludes on a point which has great relevance for teachers and which seems to offer further support for Burt when he asserts: 'Abilities are continually shifting and developing, becoming diversified or interconnected, depending on people's education and their out-of-school experience and they can be classified and sub-classified in a multitude of ways.' Or, as Burt (11) concludes: 'This supplementary factor [productive imagination] is not to be regarded as a simple faculty or "primary ability"; it is itself highly complex, and capable of further factorisations into a number of constituent sub-factors.' These views can be interpreted for the practising teacher as showing the need to be aware of the complexity of creative functioning. If teachers realise that identification of creative children may involve them in reappraising their ideas of the concepts of both creativity and giftedness, they may be well on the way to recognising creative ability. Having recognised it, they can then refine their views on how to cater for it, and encourage it.

MEASUREMENT OF CREATIVITY

Probably the most comprehensive development of creativity assessment in children has been made by Torrance and his associates working in Minnesota. For this purpose, Torrance (93) has developed the Minnesota Tests of Creative Thinking. These are described in detail by Goldman (34) and relevant parts are included in Chapter 4, together with scoring procedures. They consist of a battery of both verbal and non-verbal tests. One of the main problems concerning these tests has been that of RELIABILITY, VALIDITY and the whole problem of CRITERIA.

The term 'reliability', when applied to tests, refers to the degree to which the test will yield similar results when given at different times to the same or similar candidates. If all the children in the sample scored exactly the same score on the second administration it would imply perfect correlation. This very rarely occurs. The measure of a test's consistency is assessed in terms of a correlation coefficient. This is an index which ranges from $+1 \cdot 0$ (perfect agreement), through $0 \cdot 0$ (no agreement either way), to $-1 \cdot 0$ (negative or inverse agreement).

Test validity is the extent to which a test measures what it is intended or purports to measure, which is determined by the correlation between its results and some other criterion of what it was devised to measure. The index used is again a correlation coefficient. The real problem of validity of creativity tests is to find an acceptable measure to use as a criterion. For a fuller description of reliability and validity, the reader is referred to *Statistics in Education*, by W. H. King (Macmillan. Basic Books in Education Series), pp. 137–9.

Torrance and Gowan (98) reported for their creativity tests reliability coefficients between $0 \cdot 75$ and $0 \cdot 85$, and concluded that these were high enough to encourage further work with the material. Yamamoto (113) has developed further experimental scoring manuals for these tests and has experimental data using a variety of weighted scoring systems. Some of these procedures are also included in Chapter 4.

Goldman (34) and Goldman and Clarke (35) have reported on problems of test reliability. Goldman and Clarke looked particularly at subjective interpretation of written material. They concluded that high levels of reliability in judgements of creative writing could be obtained for individuals and between independent assessors so long as the criteria for scoring was clearly understood. The writers, in common with other investigators, urge caution in the use of these assessments. It should be pointed out that this inquiry used very small sample groups ($N = 13$ and

$N = 10$). They also quote work by Burgart, Palmer and Taylor which they contend supports their findings.

The problem of criteria is a fundamental one in research into creativity. What criterion does a teacher use to rate a model, a painting, movement or creative writing? This is a real difficulty. The work reported in Chapter 3 attempting to rate these things, was based on work reported by Sprecher in Taylor and Barron (89) and Taylor (88). These studies analyse in detail the variables involved in the criteria for creativity and are guided by the report of the Criterion Committee of the third (1959) University of Utah conference on the identification of creative talents.

There are different measures of validity which can be used to assess how well a test measures what it purports to measure. One of these is PREDICTIVE VALIDITY. This is the degree to which the test is able to predict later success in the area the test is supposed to measure. In creativity tests, as has been shown, it is difficult to find an acceptable criterion against which to assess the test.

Another measure is CONSTRUCT VALIDITY. A construct is a psychological attribute or quality of people which will be reflected in test performance. If the test in question can be analysed to demonstrate the presence of this quality or construct, this is an indication of its construct validity.

Perhaps the most obvious measure, though, is FACE VALIDITY, when it appears from the items that it really does measure what it is said to measure. (For example, to the average parent a page full of sums would obviously be measuring arithmetical ability.)

Validity studies carried out by Anderson (2) indicate that predictive validity for creativity tests is poor. Anderson puts forward the view that, by its nature, creativity is often not suitable for predictive validity studies. He also reports construct validity procedures carried out by Barron, who reported validity coefficients of 0·5 between ratings and tests of originality, and Drevdahl, who quotes even lower coefficients, but, in spite of the relatively poor validity figures quoted, Vernon (99) (revised edition, 1962) sees the work of Barron and Drevdahl as providing some external confirmation of validity – namely, promising positive correlations between tests of creativity and ratings.

Charles (14) reviewed validation studies and concluded that the use of pencil and paper or situational tests of creativity may be severely questioned on validation grounds. He could not find evidence that they would predict creative behaviour in later life. This point of view is not accepted uncritically by me, and some of the tests I devised were directed at clarifying this problem. I decided Charles's main objection to the tests as predictors was not wholly relevant to the everyday work of teachers in schools.

Both Wallach and Kogan (106) and Hudson (49) have questioned the concept of a 'test' of creativity and use of time-limits and group administrations. They catered for these objections by developing frames of reference not using these features. However, a 'task context' is inevitable and Smith (84), reviewing Hudson's work, wonders whether he has started yet another typology which may eventually be criticised as Hudson himself admonished the mental testing movement. Ward's (108) work also supported the views of Hudson and Wallach and Kogan on the concept of creativity 'testing', and teachers may wish to take account of these changing attitudes in measurement. Further support for Wallach and Kogan (106) is offered by Cropley (19), who reports that their tests had a 'high degree of internal consistency and relative independence of intelligence tests'.

CHARACTERISTICS OF THE CREATIVE PERSONALITY

As with other areas in the field of creativity, the last decade has seen a wealth of research into the characteristics of creative people. A major part of this work has been concerned with scientific creativity emanating from commercial and political needs and motives. Other work has been concerned with artistic and humanistic components, but there has not been too much attention paid to the personality characteristics of creative children. It is essential to sound a note of caution in generalising from studies with adults to expectations from children. The work with adults reviewed here has been selected because it appeared to have some relevance for teachers and where it subsequently generated further research with children.

One of the leaders in this aspect of the work has been Taylor, whose biennial conferences at the University of Utah have provided a vehicle for communication of research in this field. The personality characteristics of creative persons are described by Taylor (88) as

autonomous, self-sufficient, independent in judgements, more open to the irrational, more stable, more feminine, dominant, self-assertive, complex, more self-accepting, more resourceful and adventurous, more radical (Bohemian), self-controlled, emotionally sensitive, introverted and bold.

This list seems to summarise reports of many specific inquiries, and subsequent work reviewed looks in more detail at some of the traits mentioned by Taylor. Before this is done, however, an interesting overlap can be seen between the above list and that produced by MacKinnon (61) from studies made at the Institute of Personality Assessment and Measurement (IPAR) at the University of California as follows:

They are intelligent, original, independent in thought and action, open to experience both of the inner self and the outer world, intuitive, aesthetically sensitive and free from crippling restraints. They have high energy level, a persistent commitment to creative endeavour and a strong sense of destiny which includes a degree of resoluteness and a measure of egotism.

He also, somewhat naturally, takes the view that if a person has the minimum of intelligence required for the mastery of a field of knowledge, whether he performs creatively or banally in that field will be crucially determined by non-intellectual factors. Mention by MacKinnon of 'minimum of intelligence required' does show the links which he recognises between a personality and a cognitive approach to the study of creativity. This multi-sided approach to the problem will be characteristic of the teacher's approach to the identification of creative children.

Before an attempt is made to collate and relate these findings, one more overall view of the creative personality, that of Barron (4), is given for comparative purposes. Reporting on IPAR research with writers, architects and mathematicians, he finds the creative person more comfortable with disorder and more challenged to find a subtle way of reordering. He is more independent of judgement, more troubled about the world and has more resources for dealing with his troubles. His world is more complex, he is healthier and has more available energy. He is more open to impulse and fantasy and can 'regress in the service of the ego'.

The picture emerging from these three broad descriptions is one of a nature open to experience; having resourceful conscientiousness and sensitivity which can be further expressed in a personal, creative manner. This is not unlike the picture of the creative personality which emerged from my own research, where the profile was one of SENSITIVITY, INTROVERSION, TENDER-MINDEDNESS, CONSCIENTIOUSNESS and APPREHENSION, a picture having something in common with all three descriptions and showing as much overlap with each as they exhibit amongst themselves. I have found the work of Nelson (71) helpful in interpreting the concept of the creative personality. He gives a timely caution in matters of interpretation when he says:

There are many ways in which creative talents are discovered and encouraged, many avenues of development, and characteristics to describe people having these abilities. However, no pat, all-inclusive description will fit and describe all, and no set of descriptions will be applicable to each individual.

Rogers (81) uses a personality approach in his attempt to elucidate a theory of creativity. He stresses the ability to toy with materials, and the capacity to be puzzled, as creative personality attributes. I certainly noticed these attributes in children engaged on a wide range of creative activities. Mary, aged 11 years, had not begun to work on her model. I asked her if anything was wrong. 'I really need just to practise with the things to see how they can fit together before I decide what I can make best.' she said, illustrating Rogers's point very succinctly.

McGuire (66) and Drevdahl (24) both stress attributes highlighted in my own study. These are the need for conscientiousness and apprehensiveness in approaching creative problem-solving. Like Mary, Robert, aged 11 years, was also apprehensive. He said, 'You have to be careful. If you cut the cloth and it doesn't fit, you've ruined it.' McGuire (66) further suggests three personality dimensions significant to mental health. These are (*a*) relaxed outgoing optimism, (*b*) creatively intelligent autonomy and (*c*) self-disciplined stability. These findings seem to suggest that a link between intelligence and creative performance in mentally healthy children does exist.

In a recent study of art students and teachers, Cross, Cattell and Butcher (20) found themselves in considerable agreement with earlier work in temperamental aspects of creativity. They suggest that their study shows a higher anxiety level in artists than has been indicated in earlier studies. In their inquiry, artists are assessed as being slightly introverted, strongly anxious, experimenting, non-moralistic and slightly sensitive. Again, there is a reasonable amount of overlap between this view and others and a consensus view of the creative personality does begin to build up.

Torrance (95) reports some of his earlier work examining creative children and their classroom activities. He found that creative children, as identified by his tests, were often seen by peers as 'naughty' and having 'wild and silly ideas'. Teachers rejected the characteristics of creative children and there appeared to be poor orientation between these children and their teachers. Highly creative children seemed to create problems for the teacher in a somewhat controlled classroom situation. The original work reported by Torrance in this paper formed the basis of the decisions regarding criteria for the peer, self- and teacher-ratings of creativity described in Chapter 5.

Getzels and Jackson (32) also revealed that teachers preferred their intelligence group to the creative group. The latter was characterised by wide-ranging interests, sense of humour and emotional stability. As stated earlier, this work has been widely criticised on both sampling and methodological grounds, but Torrance (96) replicated this work eight times, and on seven occasions showed similar results. Again, one notices emotional stability featuring in yet another inquiry as an aspect of the creative personality.

A widely quoted view of the creative personality is that given by Torrance (93) where he lists eighty-four characteristics, culled from an extensive review of literature and found to differentiate highly creative persons from less creative ones. This check list has been the basis for much subsequent work on refining the concept of the creative personality. One such development is quoted by Torrance (96), who used 'The Ideal Pupil Check List', developed from the former work quoted, in cross-cultural studies of the creative personality. It emerged that the ideal creative personality differed widely from culture to culture. Perhaps this can be interpreted as another caution (similar to the one reported by Nelson) against generalisation in this field until a more rigid control of such variables as motivation, aspiration and the teacher can be obtained in an experimental situation.

SELF, PEER AND TEACHER RATINGS OF CREATIVITY

Self, peer and teacher ratings of creativity have been widely investigated in both the actual assessments of creativity and in attempts to establish predictive validity for other instruments purporting to test creative performance. Stein (85) reports work by Cattell as early as 1906 using judgements of people qualified to report on the work of others. He also reports work by Roe on similar lines in the early 1950s. Thurstone (92) suggests the use of rating and rating scales to identify creative persons, and this approach was followed by Stein and Meer (reported by Gowan (36)). From these studies it emerged that the validity of rating scales depended on the quality of the instructions given to the raters, various HALO EFFECTS, the standards set and the help given to the raters. The halo effects in ratings seems to be a particular hazard, the effects of which I noted in my study, and were also noted by Eysenck (26).

Holland (48) assessed teacher ratings as predictors of creativity, but found them more useful as predictors of academic achievements and leadership potential than as predictors of creativity.

Finding the Getzels and Jackson criteria for teacher ratings unacceptable, Richards, Clive and Needham (76) asked their teachers to rate traits where 'creatives' should score higher than 'high I.Q. types'. These results did not indicate that teachers generally favoured 'intelligent' over 'creative' pupils and the results did not confirm Getzels and Jackson's findings. They also

c

found that self-ratings were less satisfactory than teacher ratings as criteria for creativity.

Hart (45), reported by Gowan (36), compared creativity tests from the Minnesota battery with ratings, but found little relationship between the two. Similar findings are reported by Torrance (95). Burt (13), reporting earlier work of his, suggests teacher ratings are a most reliable measure of children's general social adjustment and may be related to the personality factors of EXTRAVERSION and NEUROTICISM. It is interesting to compare the comparative success of teacher ratings in predicting social adjustment and their failure to identify creative children as defined by tests.

McIntyre, Morrison and Sutherland (67) investigated teachers' assessments of primary school pupils in both social and educational spheres. Teachers' estimates seemed to be heavily biased towards good behaviour, attainments and attitudes to school: findings which are often quoted by Torrance, and hardly indicative of an approach which will lead to the identification of creative talent. Torrance (95) has studied teacher's ratings of children in American elementary schools and is concerned that teachers seem to reject the characteristics of highly creative children and seem unable to identify them. Mention has already been made of Torrance's 'Ideal Pupil Check List'. Use of this (Torrance (96)) supported Torrance's other work quoted by disclosing teachers' hostility to creativity.

PEER NOMINATIONS OF CREATIVITY have been tried, but researches all seem to have found that they do present many problems, the foremost of which appears to be the inability of children to appraise creative thinking abilities as set out in questionnaires. Getzels and Jackson (32) used peer ratings and found them affected by 'halo'; Torrance (93) noticed peer pressures towards conformity reflected in the ratings. In fact, this peer pressure of conformity is one of the factors he uses to account for the 'fourth-grade slump' in creativity which he noted. In my study there was a suggestion that peer opinion would associate conformity with 'school work' of an academic, verbal character, whilst creativity was seen in a more 'creative' capacity, and associated with non-verbal school activities.

Yamamoto (114) highlights limitations of peer ratings. He gave two tests of creative thinking to 428 high-school subjects and a peer nomination form to assess creativity. Fluency, flexibility and inventive-level scores were obtained. All the test scores and peer nominations were correlated and the results were found to be very wide-ranging, correlations from -0.85 to $+0.65$ being reported. No firm indication of the value of peer nominations as criteria for creative measures was obtained. In view of the wide-ranging correlations reported and the differing opinions held about the relative value of peer opinions as an indication of creative performance, I decided to include them in my study, but to increase the information collected to include a nomination for popularity, leadership and conformity as well. These results are discussed in Chapter 6.

Self-rating of creativity has been evaluated by many of the investigators already quoted using non-test methods of identification of creative talent. Taylor (88) used self-reports of activities and analysed these to try to elicit creative pursuits. Torrance (93) used his check list of the creative personality as the basis of a self-report study. He attempts (Torrance 95) a tentative conceptualisation of the creative child which postulated that he/she must be able to maintain the position of being 'a minority of one'.

A slightly unusual approach to the problem of self-rating in the creativity field was adopted by Cheong (15). He identified experimental pupils by asking children what kind of teachers they would like to have and then grouped the sample on their responses, taking Dewey's philosophy of experimentation as a criterion. He reports a correlation of $+0.82$ between creativity and pupils' experimental attitude – suggesting that pupils who were high in experimental attitude were most likely to be high in creativity, and vice versa. The value of this work to teachers is the importance it attaches to experimental attitude. This willingness to experiment may characterise some creative children and be a means of identifying them.

Self-rating procedures have presented severe problems to most investigators and results obtained to date are not over-encouraging. This approach is also discussed in detail in Chapter 6.

SEX DIFFERENCES IN CREATIVITY

Guilford (42), May (65) and Yamamoto (115) all examined possible sex differences in creativity in their studies. They concluded that there were no sex differences on the measures they used. There is little evidence of any sex differences being recorded. Torrance has reported work where there has been limited differences on the Minnesota Tests of Creative Thinking and Wonderley (112) also produced similar evidence. Where differences have been recorded, it has usually been as a result of the application of either a different approach or through differential rewarding systems. Torrance (96) illustrates this aspect over many fields of creative endeavour.

CREATIVITY AND SOCIAL CLASS

Over the past decade, teachers have been made very aware of educational differences which may be related to SOCIAL CLASS. Sociologists have instanced the educational disadvantages which can occur because of socio-economic differences in children's home backgrounds. They may well ask, in these circumstances, 'What is the relationship between creativity and social class?' Nuss (72) and Rivlen (79) report that highly creative pupils, as identified by tests and nomination, came from higher social-class groups than low creatives.

Wallach and Kogan (106) report that their sample came almost entirely from the upper social-class groups. It can be inferred from the work of Hudson (49) – 'I have tested in . . . five public boarding schools, one public day school, and two grammar schools' – that his sample was predominantly from the upper social class groups. Similarly, by their method of selection of sample, Getzels and Jackson (32) would not have a representative sample of the complete social-class range. It appears that a wide range of studies have not used samples which could throw light on this problem, and in view of this I decided to study the relationship between social class and creativity. The approach was largely unproductive, but I could find no evidence that creative ability, as measured by a variety of tests and ratings, was in any way significantly related to the social class of the parents of the children in the sample.

SUMMARY

The chapter discusses various ideas on the nature of creativity. Some of these are seen to have more particular relevance for the work of teachers and interpretation of this work is suggested.

Psychological views on the relationship of creativity to intelligence are discussed in some detail. Basically, the discussion centres on whether creativity is part of what is commonly called 'intelligence', or whether it is a separate mode of cognitive functioning, which is separate from intelligence.

Some of the problems of measuring creativity are discussed. These are principally, 'Do creativity tests really measure creativity, do they give similar results when given on different occasions, and by what yard-stick do we assess whether any act is creative?'

The characteristics of the creative personality are probably many and varied but such attributes as sensitivity, tender-mindedness, emotional stability and an ability to remain uncommitted and receptive to experiences seem to be important.

Self, peer and teacher ratings of creativity are reviewed, but seem to be unreliable.

There seems to have been little research to investigate whether creative ability is associated more strongly with one social-class group than another. An attempt to assess this was largely unproductive, but there was no evidence that creativity was related to the social class of the parents of the children studied.

FURTHER READING

Fruchter, B. *Introduction to Factor Analysis* (Van Nostrand 1954)

King, W. H. *Statistics in Education* (Macmillan. Basic Books in Education Series 1969)

McKellar, P. *Imagination and Thinking. A Psychological Analysis* (Cohen & West 1957)

Most of the books on the Basic Reading List given after the Introduction would constitute useful follow-up reading from this chapter.

2 Creativity in young children – some basic considerations

> The conscious nurture of children's creative potentialities may still be a worthwhile operation, but not because it produces more and better brain-workers. It may be worthwhile because, quite simply, it makes school a more enjoyable place to be.
>
> LIAM HUDSON (49)

The aim of this chapter is to examine some fundamentals which impinge on decisions teachers must make regarding their professional role. Torrance (93) has shown that both the educational system and teachers themselves are punitive towards children showing creative potential. When one looks objectively at the work of the teacher, however, it becomes increasingly clear that no one is in a better position either to identify or to guide and encourage such children.

CREATIVITY AND THE TEACHER'S PERSONAL PHILOSOPHY

Fleming (27) has analysed the work of the teacher in great detail. From this analysis it emerges that, prior to beginning their professional work, most teachers have begun to think in terms of the formulation of a personal philosophy of teaching. This is simple and practical at first; almost an act of survival, when the basic questions asked are, 'Have I something to teach?' and 'How can teaching best be done?' It is when these questions are seen against a backcloth of the young teacher's professional training and the situation found in schools that the personal philosophy begins to develop. It becomes refined by more perceptive insight into how young children learn, and heightened by an awareness of individual and group problems. It is further deepened when the teacher feels a degree of concern that perhaps the emphasis on 'teaching' in his initial questions was misplaced, and that the primary question which should have been asked was: 'How can I arrange for children to learn?'

During a teacher's professional training, the psychological, philosophical and sociological bases of education are examined in detail, and links are made between these and practice in school. The basis on which decisions of organisation, curriculum and general school planning are made is discussed. What are the reasons for doing things in a certain way? Is there any evidence from the theory and research which suggests that a particular approach is desirable? Although students follow these arguments and discussions with enthusiasm and diligence, they seem to take place in a vacuum. It is only when the student takes up his first appointment that his personal philosophy takes on a dynamic, changing and evolving nature. In school, as a member of the teaching team, he is able to weigh the evidence more effectively against the criteria of what he finds he is able to handle, and what he assesses to be successful. In short, he becomes involved in issues which affect his professional life. MacDonald (60) maintains that an element of involvement, governed by temperament rather than intellect is virtually inevitable in someone concerned with discussing philosophies of education. He suggests that a professional preparation enables the teacher to think about both the 'how' and 'what' of education by introducing him to the best which has been said about the topics, and concludes that this should have done more than raise the level of his practitioner's intuition: it should have enabled the teacher to enhance his work through objective reflection, free from a partisan attitude.

If the teacher is to cater adequately for the creative thinking abilities of children, his personal philosophy must be one which values the individuality of the child, recognises that the basis of education lies in the emotions and conceives that most children can be regarded as potentially gifted in some sphere if only it can be identified. With regards to the latter point, it is pertinent to note that Guilford (41) presents specific evidence on this when he says:

In an ordinary kind of population, Bloom (7) found that if we were to define as 'gifted' a child who is in the highest 10% on any one of Thurstone's Primary Mental Abilities tests, as many as 60% could be regarded as gifted. If the number of tests was increased to extend the range of intellectual factors involved, the percentage might approach 100, reminding us that where abilities differ in kind, and the number is large, almost any child can be 'gifted' in something.

This belief enables the teacher to proceed from the assumption that there is a likelihood of the learning experiences he provides, if they are varied enough, being able to provide the impetus for most children to extend some of them in a creative way. The message from Bloom's work, using Thurstone's tests, is simply that when the number of different abilities is large, there is room for extremely wide individual variation. Teachers need to be constantly aware that even in the most seemingly homogeneous group there will be tremendous individual differences, and the ultimate aim must be to try to stimulate these abilities by planning individual tasks, often within experiences presented to groups.

Basically, teachers need to be fully aware that creativity is concerned with a very complex series of cognitive and emotional variables which are dependent for their development upon an individual's potential and experience. The teacher's contact with the child is a very powerful agent in determining the way in which individuals will use their talents, controlling as it does, to some extent, both the type of experience provided and the amount of effort which is applied, and which is shown in the degree of involvement reached.

THE ROLE OF THE TEACHER AND THE IMPLICATIONS FOR OPTIMUM FULFILMENT OF CREATIVE POTENTIAL

Teaching of the kind intended here is not a brutal imposition, but the creation of an independence of authority through coming to share concepts and apply the same impersonal procedures of validation as those of the teacher. Such a liberalised kind of teaching does not just tell, though it has a place for that too. It questions, discusses, sets tasks, hints, preserves judicious silences, prompts, provokes, invites contradictions, feigns ignorance, poses problems, demonstrates, pretends perplexity, comments, explains and so on through the battery of devices by means of which passivity in intellectual learning may be overcome and a more critical learning stimulated.

In the above quotation, Dearden (22) suggests for the teacher a very complex role. His aim here is to achieve a liberalisation of teaching. I believe that a teacher adopting these techniques would be going a long way towards effectively helping to encourage and extend the creative thinking of children. By using these methods, he would be keeping the child both receptive to ideas and reflective about them. He would be producing a situation which would engage the children and invite creative thought by presenting possibilities for the individual transformation of ideas presented as an initial stimulus.

Freeman, Butcher and Christie (28) review many pieces of research concerning how teachers can help creative children. They conclude that 'creative development can be enhanced through the use of discovery methods', and stress that both home and school environments should give 'free rein and a ready response to the explorations of the child'. This last quotation highlights a real dilemma of the teacher. There is a need to give children free rein for both adventurous activities and original thought, but there is an implication of teacher interaction in the phrase 'ready response'. This dual aspect is important. Children need freedom to be engrossed in an activity of their choice, but they also require a mentor and guide on many occasions. This apparent paradox is illustrated in many classrooms where the teacher is removed and yet present, concerned and yet not an inhibitor, the provider of some ideas and yet the elicitor of more. The teacher who successfully blends these paradoxical aspects will be likely to produce pupils who will be adventurous, and yet able to step outside and objectively evaluate their efforts. They will be free and yet secure, outwardly uninhibited and yet inwardly acquiring a more acute self-knowledge.

In order to cater effectively for the children to maximise their creative potential, it seems that the teacher becomes not only a collector of resources, but something more. He becomes an educational cartographer who selects wide areas from which the children choose appropriate sections to make their own individual maps.

Williams (110), working in Minnesota, shows the need for teachers to having training in the identification of highly creative pupils and how to cater for their subsequent development. Little specific work in this direction has yet been done in this country, but it appears that the strategies most frequently used to develop divergent thinking by American teachers in Williams's sample are often used intuitively by teachers everywhere. These include attempts to increase the ability to express oneself in a variety of media; thinking of a variety of possible solutions to a problem; evaluating ideas and situations calling for opinion, choice and judgement; provocative questioning to encourage original lines of thinking; making links between past knowledge and present problems; and arranging for the acquisition of the skills involved in finding relevant material.

A most important factor in encouraging children to use their creative abilities is that the teacher should really believe that all pupils are capable of achieving a high level of creative functioning. In psychological terms, 'teacher expectation must be high'. Rosenthal and Jacobson (82) produce amazing evidence regarding teacher expectation. They reported to teachers that, as a result of a special test, they had been able to identify children who during the next twelve months would show unusual potential for intellectual growth. The names of these children had, in fact, been drawn at random. Eight months later these unusual or 'magic' children (those predicted as 'bloomers') showed significantly greater gains in I.Q. than did the remaining children, who had not been singled out for the teacher's attention. The change in the teacher's expectations regarding the intellectual performance of these allegedly 'special' children had led to an actual change in the intellectual performance of these randomly selected children. Rosenthal and Jacobson suggest, from their work, that the teacher's role is one of Pygmalion in the classroom: 'The difference between a lady and a flower-girl is not how she behaves but how she's treated.' If the teacher expects children to achieve high levels of creative ability, there is great likelihood that they will do so. However, they do discuss other experimental work regarding the effects of teacher's self-fulfilling prophecies (p. 57). Only two main studies had preceded theirs, and results from these had produced evidence which was both supporting and damaging to their hypotheses. They discuss the possible reasons for the results which did not support their work, and suggest that these may have been due to the experimental design, which did not control the teacher variable. Although they present formidable evidence to support their findings, they do acknowledge that additional evidence would be useful in this field.

Sometimes a cautionary tale helps to illustrate a point. A group of 10-year-old boys of mixed ability were working on a mathematical assignment. They had a wealth of apparatus and structural material and their lines of enquiry were guided by two assignment cards. Alan, a boy of average ability, was reading a card. He said, 'What does parallel mean?' The teacher stood by and was tempted to intervene to help with the question, but more especially to reprimand Roy (I.Q. 85), who was looking out of the window, apparently day-dreaming. Luckily, she waited, and after what appeared to be an age Roy turned to Alan, whose question had not been answered and said, 'You can tell what parallel is like if you look out of the window at the sides of the blocks of flats over there.' He went on to extend his observations. He had a clear understanding of what 'parallel' meant but needed help with the verbalising of his ideas. The teacher now stepped in and helped him with his explanation. What had appeared to be day-dreaming had in fact been very relevant thinking. The tendency to act too quickly can sometimes prevent individual thought. This example illustrates the need to wait, and shows the opportune moment when the teacher can be particularly helpful.

One of the best-known experiments (8) with highly creative children in England was carried out at Brentwood College of Education as part of a study of all types of gifted children. An important aim of this work was to explore ways in which creative thinking could be stimulated in the classroom. Some children were selected on the results of certain tests of creativity and the ratings of experts in creative subjects. They proved to range in I.Q. from 120 to 157, and in this respect were not unlike Getzels and Jackson's samples of highly creative children. It is suggested in the report of this work that the results are guides for further action, rather than in any way definitive. Several implications for the teacher are, however, suggested. Creative children need real challenge built into the stimulus which the teacher provides: involvement was increased in their children when ideas for following up were novel. If the starting-point was effective and full of creative possibilities, children had no difficulty in developing their own ideas from it. They became immediately committed to the work and maintained a high interest level throughout. The children in this sample were self-contained within their own productive activity and not easily distracted by their neighbours. This is a frequent observation of teachers working with children in the 8–13 years age range and must stem from the involvement in an activity having a real intrinsic interest for the child. The intuitive nature of the teacher's role in dealing with creative children is well-documented by this report, which concludes:

The lesson that our students need to learn above all others, is that one can really appreciate how much success one is having as a teacher by developing a kind of invisible antenna which can be turned in to every little happening in the class: the expression on a child's face, the overheard snatch of conversation, the degree of involvement with which a child is working.

Hildreth (47) also presents a comprehensive picture of the creative child as part of a study of the gifted child in a wider context. She highlights the role of the teacher as 'mentor': one who excites the child and fosters his tendencies towards exploration. This kind of teacher opens up new avenues of interest, demonstrates new techniques of working or performing, shows how great minds have thought, helps the child to evaluate his work. His role is the opposite of teaching by fiat: 'First you do this, then follow by that and this will give you the answer.' The gifted teacher of the creative, in Hildreth's terms, is 'a true guide to the perplexed'.

The work of Torrance (93) has become something of a classic in this field. His theme is concerned with the guidance of creative talent. The following ideas are suggested by him for encouraging creativity in children in school:

(*a*) Encourage unusual questions.

(*b*) Reward creative effort in the form of unusual and imaginative ideas.

(*c*) Show the pupils that you value their ideas.

(*d*) Allow some activities to develop without evaluation.

(*e*) Avoid setting tasks on the basis of 'boys do this and girls do that'.

(*f*) Do not judge a child by his success in reading and writing. A creative child may lag behind.

(*g*) Encourage experimentation, spontaneity and the utilisation of errors for further learning.

There is a constant thread running through the suggestions made by most researchers concerned with how to assist in the fulfilment of creative potential in children. This is that school experiences should involve the children more positively in the whole process of education – in questioning, listening, discussing, thinking and being actively involved in practical working with a wide variety of materials. This involvement will be achieved by a personal relationship based on trust and respect for each other as individuals, where each contributes significantly to the partnership, the teacher ultimately helping in the 'conversion of accustomed knowledge to the unaccustomed idea, product or act'. (90).

THE NEED FOR SELF-ACTUALISATION AND HOW THE TEACHER CAN ENHANCE THIS

The term 'self-actualisation' is used extensively by Maslow (64). He distinguishes between 'special talent creativeness' and 'self-actualising creativeness'. The former he associates with standard and conventionally accepted areas of creative endeavour, such as poems, novels, theories, experiments and paintings. The latter he sees springing more directly from the personality and showing itself in attempts to do anything creatively. For example, the teacher who employs the unusual technique, the spontaneous idea, who frees himself from the stereotyped approach, and is adventurous in his expectations is the type of person Maslow has described as 'self-actualising'. He is a person who is realising his own creative potential, and in doing so may provide the kind of environment which encourages creative responses in the children. Maslow suggests that this is because he has resolved some of his inner conflicts and as a consequence has more of himself available for creative use. 'He wastes less of his time and energy protecting himself against himself.'

This idea of 'self-actualisation' is seen in the work of many writers, but it may appear in different guises. Anderson (2) sees it as synonymous with health or the fullest humanness, Rogers (80) sees it in people who are 'open to experience' and 'fully functioning'. Fromm (29) shows the need for the individual to be stable and free from neurotic distortions, and to have a degree of inner maturity. But he proposes that in order to respond creatively in a situation there must be complete relatedness, in which both parties (in our case, the teacher and the pupil) 'become one, although at the same time they remain two. . . . One transcends the boundaries of his own person, and at the very moment when he feels "I am" he also feels "I am you", I am one with the whole world.' I think this is once more the situation described by Reid (75) as one of affinity, 'where the teacher and the child are open to each other'. The suggestion is made that this is the real teaching moment, when the teacher can intuitively guide the child towards his own achievement of a measure of self-actualisation. It is from a rapport of this kind that the child is likely to develop a more perceptive knowledge of the complexities of his environment, and to discover and manipulate new relationships, using his own individual strategies. In this way the child becomes more aware of his own potentialities and successes, through intrinsic motivation, which leads to a degree of the self-actualisation we are discussing here.

Working with a group of boys during the assessment of creative ability in model-making, I talked to Tony, aged 10, about his model which looked like a horse. 'Would it have so many legs?' (It appeared to have five.) He looked at the model rather deliberately, as if for the first time analytically. After a pause, he said to me with some disdain, 'That piece [which appeared to be the fifth leg] is holding the front legs in position. Eventually this horse will be jumping over a fence and it will look right then.' I suggested a slight move of the arrangement for which there was little enthusiasm until he said, 'Now, that's given me another idea,' and he proceeded to realign the holder so that it acted as a support which gave the horse the air of jumping over a fence. I believe that this encounter had the elements suggested by both Fromm and Reid, and that it illustrates one instance of the teacher assisting an appropriate level of self-actualisation. Tony, with Taoist perception, had lost sight of the external and concentrated on the total effect. He saw what he wanted to see, the complete end product, and not the pure detail seen at first by me. However, he accepted by final comment, let it lie fallow and eventually adapted it, personally, and used it in his own individual interpretation to achieve his desired effect.

INTELLIGENCE AND CREATIVITY. THE IMPLICATIONS OF RESEARCH FINDINGS FOR THE TEACHER'S WORK IN THE CLASSROOM

The nature of creativity and its relationship to intelligence, as seen in recent research by psychologists, has been discussed extensively in Chapter 1. Here it will suffice to reiterate that, although creativity and high intelligence are positively correlated, they are by no means synonymous. A high score on an I.Q. test certainly does not mean that the same pupil will be highly creative. Torrance (95) has pointed out that the top 20 per cent of the school population on the basis of I.Q. alone tends to include only about 30 per cent of those individuals who are in the top 20 per cent on measures of creative thinking. On this reasoning the group of children regarded as academically gifted fails to include about 70 per cent of the highly creative as measured by creativity tests. The literature in this field is well documented and reviewed by both Cropley (18) and Hildreth (47). Most general books in the field of creativity report relevant research in some detail. In this chapter the aim is to examine the implications of research findings for the teacher's work in the classroom.

One of the fundamental dilemmas facing the teacher is whether he is to accept that the urge towards creativity is almost universal, or whether he is to believe that it is a special aptitude of the chosen few. There are supporters for both viewpoints, but most researchers agree basically with the Guilford (40) view that 'Creativity is not a special gift of the select few. It is, indeed, a property shared by all humanity, to a greater or lesser degree.' If the teacher accepts this view, the implication is surely that the classroom organisation needs to be such that all the children have the opportunity to realise their creative ability to its fullest potential. It may be interpreted as a plea for flexibility of organisation: an arrangement which would allow the individual to develop his own particular interests in a manner most suited to his own approach to creative problem-solving. It could be argued that it is a pointer towards widening the whole concept of the curriculum to include pursuits which would appeal to a wider range of pupils. If the curriculum is defined in terms of academic subjects, this may preclude the potentially creative gardener or creative cook from experimenting in these areas. It could mean that, because they were not introduced to gardening or cookery, the creative urge and ability in these subjects was never fully realised. The teacher is often in a position to decide in which areas it is possible to be creative by either withholding or granting subject options. In this way he may either encourage or preclude pupils from taking part in creative pursuits. This is a real responsibility; one which requires thought, discussion and objective assessment. Maslow (64) suggested, in this context, that 'a first-rate soup is more creative than a second rate painting'. Teachers need to consider issues such as this in making decisions concerning curriculum planning.

If the criterion for excellence is academic ability alone, then many children will fail to distinguish themselves. If the criteria for excellence include a wide range of abilities, then more children may achieve distinction. Certainly, if the view that 'Agility of mind is of more use in a changing world than enduring subject-matter' is accepted, the curriculum must be characterised by a wide range of choices and options. Training in 'how to think' will assume far more importance than the body of knowledge to be learned. In other words, the process of learning will take preference over the end-product.

The tendency towards mixed-ability groupings is now widespread in primary education, and indeed, the movement towards inter-disciplinary inquiry (I.D.E.) in secondary schools has been accompanied by a move away from ability groups in the secondary field as well. This presents a great challenge, but it also presents a great opportunity. In terms of catering for the individual, it means that teachers, whether they be class teachers, subject specialists or middle-school consultant/advisers, are going to be faced with children having very varied ability backgrounds. In this situation, it is important for the teacher to recognise that the stimuli used in arranging for children's learning are to be such that they elicit a wide variety of responses. Provision needs to be made for children of high academic ability to have headway built into their work to extend them, whilst less able children are provided with a situation which involves problem-solving appropriate to their interests. The latter need the impetus towards creative thinking, so that through the ensuing self-directed activity the skilful teacher will be able to extend work, not only in the creative sphere, but in fundamental skills as well.

My own research suggests that creativity does not exist as a single-group factor or entity. Rather, there are indications of a number of separate group factors, each concerned with specific areas of creative activities. This is at variance with much of the Guilford inspired research in America, which implied that 'creativity' and 'intelligence' are terms that appropriately label unified but different psychological dimensions of comparable generality. It is, however, compatible with more recent work carried out in this field by Wodtke (111), Marsh (63) and Lovell and Shields (59), who doubt the independence of creativity and intelligence. Lovell and Shields (59), in particular, paralleled the findings of my research. They claimed that creative activities 'seemed to fragment'. This certainly happened in my study, where the creative activities each appeared as separate factors, seeming to require an ability appropriate to each area under review. Different abilities were required for creative writing, model-making, painting, drama and physical activities. The implication of this finding for the teacher is further support for the idea of a widening, expanding and flexible curriculum. Lovell and Shields (59) again support this inference. They state: 'Divergent thinking cannot be accounted for by one dimension; rather, the able pupil

D

is "creative" to different degrees according to the task set him.'
From observational evidence I collected, it would seem that where
interest and motivation were high, children tended to perform
better in creative activities. Wall (104, 105), in articles specifically
concerned with gifted children, added to this when postulating
that creativity is likely to result from a well-stored mind and a
certain fineness of perception. It seems that teachers should
encourage intrinsic interest in any sphere, help the child to
acquire both knowledge and skill in the area, and so give the wide
background from which creative generalisations can be made.
Vernon's (100) work is also relevant to this point. He regards
intelligence as a fluid collection of infinitely varied thinking
abilities and quarrels with Guilford's structure of intellect model,
which he thinks carries to extremes the breaking down of intelligence into different components. 'Abilities', he says, 'are continually shifting and developing, becoming diversified or interconnected, depending on people's education and their out-of-
school experiences.' To cater for these conditions is an exacting
but rewarding job for the teacher. That it is not easy is a fact. How
can it be done? That there is no black box which will provide all
the answers is also a fact. There is evidence (Cropley 18, pp. 55,
83) that a permissive and egalitarian atmosphere both at home and
at school will help to produce conditions favourable to creative
growth, but Cropley does draw attention to certain negative
properties of permissive homes as well. It seems that some basic
controls and some acceptable code of order are necessary for
children, but that these must be such that they provide an element
of individual freedom and opportunities for the exercise of choice,
judgement and risk-taking.

Much has been written regarding how the teacher can encourage creative thinking in the classroom. It is not the purpose
of this chapter to cover this ground again, but rather to conclude
this section by presenting some questions for consideration and
discussion.

QUESTIONS FOR DISCUSSION

1 The activities of the classroom conducive to creativity should be characterised by spontaneity, newness, problem-solving and inquiry without direct evaluation. How are these characteristics to be achieved within the current demands of the curriculum?

2 Is there a dichotomy between the basic need of the teacher to evaluate work done by the pupils, and the suggestion that evaluation is inhibiting to the creative child? If so, how is the dichotomy to be resolved?

3 How does the teacher achieve the conformity required to ensure good basic order and organisation and still preserve an atmosphere which encourages the creative development of individual lines of inquiry?

4 Is there a difference between the understanding of an idea and the appreciation of it? Discuss the place of these two aspects in classroom learning, and their relevant importance in children of widely differing ability.

5 Give examples of the way you have reorganised children's past experiences in relation to their present problems in order to develop new and fruitful lines of inquiry.

6 How important is it to children that their creative products are appreciated by another person?

7 'The more he strives, the less likely he is to succeed ... for the decisive idea has a way of appearing when the mind is passive and even contemplating nothing in particular' (Rosamond Harding, *An Anatomy of Inspiration*, Frank Cass & Co. 1967). Does this idea pose any problems for the teacher dealing with an unstreamed class?

8 Bearing in mind the psychological evidence regarding the relationship of intelligence and creativity, discuss the values of different forms of class organisations, e.g. unstreamed groups, team-teaching, subject-setting, groups formed by sociometric criteria, etc.

9 'The teacher's approach "invited" the children to be creative.' In what way do you think the teacher referred to in the statement may have organised her work?

10 Write down as many examples as you can which show how you acted as a (*a*) consultant, (*b*) agent, (*c*) catalyst, in producing the need to create in a child. Select suitable examples, and in a group discuss their effectiveness.

SUMMARY

The chapter stresses the importance to the teacher of developing a personal philosophy of education based on a full appreciation of the factors involved in children's learning. Some criteria are suggested which may be useful as bases from which thinking may develop. The changing role of the teacher in school today is outlined, and the implications of changing approaches for creative development are fully detailed. Examples are given of many aspects of the new role which teachers are adopting, and illustrations are used to link the discussion with classroom situations. The psychological research findings regarding intelligence and creativity are examined purely from the point of view of the practising teacher, and are assessed against the question, 'How can these findings help the teacher to be more effective and efficient?'

3 Creativity and the Curriculum

The word 'curriculum' is generally taken to refer to all school-orientated learning experiences of children. Investigators, however, do vary in their interpretation of the term. Hughes (51) uses the word to denote only planned learning experiences; he sees these as implying a statement of educational objectives, denoting desired learning outcomes in terms of student behaviour. Grobman (37), on the other hand, includes in his definition unplanned experiences which may produce results opposed to the decisions of the curriculum-planners. The movement in recent years has been towards regarding 'curriculum' in the very widest sense. Study of what is taught in schools has always concerned educators. Reference to practical accounts of schools in operation in different periods will show patterns of curriculum changes. These will usually be related to the general social climate of the era, current development in educational thought and practice, and to the growth of the fields of knowledge which are the province of the school. The emphasis in early English State elementary education on the acquisition of skill in reading, writing and arithmetic (the 3 Rs) reflects the need for a literate and numerate society based on developing industry. The 1944 Education Act changed this emphasis and anticipated the social values of an immediate post-war idealism by stressing that each child should have an education suited to his age, aptitude and ability. The move towards a comprehensive system of education in the 1960s is based on changing concepts of educability and equality of opportunity.

Progress in curriculum change is seldom uniform and steady.

There are halts, recessions, periods of latency and spurts throughout the years. The 1960s have been characterised by intense activity in the field of curriculum investigation. This has led to the 'Curriculum Development' movement, which has promoted large-scale research schemes, the establishment of teacher's centres, and an atmosphere which has encouraged all teachers to examine, in an objective manner, the aims and objectives of both the method and content of their teaching. This movement can be traced back many decades, but it was the work of Bloom (6) and his associates in Chicago in the early 1950s which systematised much of the early thinking. They carried out an exhaustive inquiry into the meanings of the verb 'to know'. Bloom believed that when we teach children we stimulate different aspects of their intelligence, and therefore it is important to know what kind of knowledge we are demanding of them, and in what ways we are testing for it. He suggested a hierarchy of learning and said that evaluation, the judgement of values, was very high in this hierarchy. Successively lower were synthesis, the production of a whole idea from parts, analysis, the breakdown of material into its elements, application, the use of principles in specific situations, comprehension, 'the lowest level of understanding', as seen in translation, interpretation, explanation or the making of summaries; and least important in the hierarchy he placed knowledge, concerned with knowing facts, classifications, etc. – often called 'cognitive memory'. Bloom and his group believed that many educators teach cognitive memory processes because these are easiest to learn and most efficiently measured. Higher processes are often neglected, to the considerable disadvantage of many children. Working initially on procedures developed by Bloom for teaching and measuring the processes he identified, other investigators have gradually produced a vast theoretical basis on which curriculum decisions can be built.

CURRICULUM DEVELOPMENT AND CREATIVITY

The more objective approaches to curriculum, whose beginnings have been outlined, have very significant relevance to children's creative development. In England this is best illustrated by looking at the work of Charity James (52) at the University of London, Goldsmiths' College. Her interest has been in the development of Inter-disciplinary Enquiry (I.D.E.) in secondary education. She is seeking 'an education in which young people are actually engaged . . . in which they are decision-makers . . . in which their perception of each other and of themselves . . . is the major concern of the collaboration process'. Introduction of this kind of education seems to be catering effectively for creative children along the lines set out in the previous chapter. James brings out clearly the value of dialogue in creative education, showing the contribution of both social and internal dialogue to adventurous thinking. If teachers understand the psychology of creative abilities, and are concerned about providing the appropriate learning experiences for them, the basis for building the curriculum suggested by James will form an admirable vehicle for them to use to clarify their aims and objectives. She highlights the need for teachers to decide when to teach what to whom, and points out that social, cultural and individual values and trends need to be taken into consideration in planning. Her final point is that schooling should be more like living. The implementation of this point should make the environment more amenable to highly creative children, who are likely to be relaxed and receptive in a less formal, less openly didactic situation.

CURRICULUM EVALUATION

A teacher who is concerned about providing learning experiences which are appropriate for creative children will naturally be interested in assessing the success of the provisions which have been made. Sometimes evaluation is considered by teachers to be synonymous with testing, but here a wider view is taken. Grobman (37) supports this line and suggests that evaluation 'includes anything relevant to judging whether the curriculum is satisfactory in terms of implementing the aims of the persons creating, adopting or adapting it, or of the society in which it exists'. In these terms evaluation can be thought of in many contexts. Visitors' reactions may be a useful assessment and the fact that other teachers decide to use similar approaches may be relevant.

These situations, although important, are relatively subjective and unstructured, and many teachers will see the need to work out evaluation techniques which have a more objective basis. Ratings by the teacher or colleagues presents one way in which this can be done. In the next section, descriptions are given of one attempt to do this. In any evaluation, a teacher will look carefully at the relevance of the criteria by which assessments are made. Are the criteria suitable for the stage of development of the children, do they reflect developmental needs, and are they related to the initial aims of the teacher? The attempt at assessment should provide some feedback and link between how the experiences have been used by the children and the carefully thought-out aims and objectives developed by the teacher when preparing the work.

In the past teachers have tended to regard any form of evaluation by 'outsiders' as an inspection of their own efficiency. This attitude is seen less and less now. There is a change of attitude in the profession which welcomes external evaluation as a chance to clarify ideas, improve techniques, and structure more efficient progression. As the concept of one teacher, one classroom, one class has broken down, much of the insularity of the teacher has disappeared. There is a greater opportunity for discussion and evaluation with colleagues and a more complex pupil/teacher interaction involving several teachers and larger groups of children. This is perhaps best illustrated in the co-operative or team teaching which is characterising much of the education of children in the middle years of schooling. Evaluation is still essential in team teaching, and is probably more effective as colleagues join forces to make assessments. Lovell (58) points out this need very strongly. He says: 'It is essential for the head and the staff to think out their educational objectives in respect to team teaching, the means whereby they hope to reach these, and the manner in which they intend to evaluate their efforts.' His emphasis is on purpose, techniques and assessment. A related view with a slightly different emphasis is given by Richmond (77). He focuses on the need for objectives to be so specific as to be readily evaluated. His view is that the teacher should have clear ideas of intended outcomes, and identify what the learner will be able to do at the end of the course. Whilst both these views are supported, it seems necessary to indicate that they do not provide a 'mutually inclusive' arrangement which precludes any deviation or inhibits creative responses outside the envisaged objectives. The open-ended nature of the provisions must be fundamentally preserved, and originality of thought encouraged and rewarded. The clear definition of aims and clinical evaluation of results should enhance, not stifle, creative potential.

ASSESSMENT OF CREATIVE ABILITY IN SELECTED AREAS OF THE CURRICULUM

Creativity and the curriculum has involved in this chapter an introduction to some ideas concerned with the content of the curriculum, Curriculum Development, and evaluation. It has been shown that evaluation can be thought of in terms of its being central to preparation, planning and organisation of work. It has also been suggested that evaluation can enhance the possibility of providing conditions where creative children can flourish. But can these creative children be identified by teachers? There is by no means any certainty that they can. The possibility of identification will be increased if teachers have a sound knowledge of the psychological bases of creativity, an understanding of the creative process and personality and an awareness of the conditions which are likely to elicit creative response. With this background, teachers may be in a position to attempt objective assessment of creative ability based on appropriate criteria.

It is the aim of this section to describe a series of attempts to evaluate creative ability over a wide range of activities normally associated with the curriculum of children during the middle years of schooling.

An attempt was made to develop rating procedures and ideas for assessment of creative ability. This work is exploratory and the findings are still very tentative. More detailed work is required in each area discussed, and many suggestions which are made will need considerable refinement and further experimental testing. They are offered here as growth-points from which the reader may develop other ideas. It is hoped that the ideas will provide material for discussion, and lead to more specific work in devising other instruments which can be used to identify creative children. This work does show, in fact, how tests can be devised, and how ideas regarding evaluation can be tried out on a more objective basis. The outlines given here are certainly not to be regarded in any way as accepted measuring instruments. It is hoped that by perusing this section, and perhaps trying out some of the ideas offered, readers will gain a greater understanding of what is meant by 'creative activities', and see how these can be extended by judicious planning to cater more effectively for the development of children's creative thinking abilities. The conceptions are presented in a spirit of sharing experience with the reader, so that they may subsequently assist him in acquiring more effective classroom procedures.

General instructions which were given to raters concerning the organisation and ranking of the work in this study are given in Appendix 2.

AN EXPLORATORY ATTEMPT TO ASSESS CREATIVE ABILITY IN MATHEMATICS

The assessment of creative ability in mathematics centred round the development of two tests, designated A and B, which I devised specifically for this purpose.

Test A is an individual test and involves placing a pack of playing-cards on a table at random. The actual instructions given are as follows:

Instructions

Place the cards at random on the table, face upwards. Say to the child: 'I would like you to pick up six cards which you think go together in any way at all. Just say why do you think they belong together when you have collected six. In this game the more sets you collect, the better. Think of as many different ways that six cards can belong together as you can. You can replace the cards on the table after selecting each set and use the cards in another set if you wish. See how many sets you can collect in five minutes. Begin.' Start counting the time as the first set is completed. If a child cannot find any sets or very few, don't use the complete time if it is obviously distressing to the child. Note down the name, class and number of sets. A set will be 'allowed' if a satisfactory reason (either logical or creative) is given.

In this study the marking instructions for test *A* were as follows:

Give one mark for each completed set indicated after having ascertained that it does constitute a 'set', and that a valid reason for assembling that set is given. The total for this test is the sum of these marks.

Test B is administered as a group test. The following information is given on a blackboard.

$$2 \qquad 3 \qquad 6$$
$$+ \qquad - \qquad \times \qquad \div$$

Instructions

'Here are seven symbols. Three are numbers, four are arithmetical signs. Read them with me. . . . Is there anyone who does not know what the signs mean? [All should know, but reinforce by going through . . . + means add, − means subtract or take away, ÷ means divide or share and × means multiply or times.]

'I want you to see how many sums you can make up, using these figures and signs. You can use as many or as few as you like, but each figure or sign can only be used *once* in each sum. You will, of course, give the answer to the sum you make up. Who can think of a sum? [Take several examples or give the following:

$$2 + 3 = \qquad 6 - 2 = \qquad 23 + 6 =$$
$$3 + 6 = \qquad 6 \div 3 =$$

'Now you see what to do. See how many sums you can make up?

(There is no time limit. In practice it is found that the experienced teacher can call a halt at the appropriate time without either penalising pupils or becoming involved in an over-lengthy test.)

The marking instructions for test B in this study were as follows:

Marking instructions

Give two marks for each sum made up and correctly answered, one mark to each acceptable sum made up but not having the correct answer, and three marks to each sum correctly answered, using more than three figures or symbols.

N.B. – Sums qualifying for marks must be recognisable arithmetical processes.

The construction of both tests was initially influenced by ideas developed by Burt (11). Discussing mathematical ability, he describes it as 'the ability to form, retain and use associations of numerical and non-verbal symbols'. Both tests were conceived within this framework, but the aim was to try to develop a form of assessment which would sample some creative aspect of mathematical ability not covered by conventional tests.

In devising the tests, I was also influenced by the work of Mackworth (62), who distinguished between problem-solvers and problem-finders, associating the former with convergent thinking and the latter with divergent thinking. In both tests, therefore, an element of making up problems or groups was an essential part.

The reliability and validity of the tests was assessed by means of the usual statistical techniques. Test re-test reliability was established as detailed in Table A.

TABLE A : *Test re-test reliability for Tests A and B*

Test	Reliability coefficient	Number in sample
A	0·88	54
B	0·85	54

Table B shows the intercorrelations between tests A, B and the N.F.E.R. Test C.1.

TABLE B : *Intercorrelations of Tests, A, B and the N.F.E.R. Test C.1*

	N.F.E.R. C.1:	Test A	Test B
N.F.E.R. C.1		0·31 (N = 49)	0·54 (N = 49)
Test A			0·31 (N = 54)

A factor analysis of the data was carried out which suggested that an element of general ability was required in performance on both tests. Various ratings by teachers were shown in the research to be distinctly associated with general scholastic ability and both tests had correlations of about 0·3 with these ratings, which, although not high, shows an important relationship, using this type of material. The same is true of the relationship between the two maths tests and creative writing variables, which were also associated with verbal intelligence. The greatest support for the suggestion that general ability is required for these tests of creative ability in mathematics comes from the factor analysis, where the tests had factor loadings of 0·392 and 0·420 respectively on the verbal intelligence factor, which accounted for the greatest amount of the variance. However, with results such as these there are indications that other qualities besides verbal intelligence are required to do these tests. Exactly what is the psychological nature of these qualities is not at all easy to determine at this stage. A great deal more research work is needed to throw more light on this problem.

There are several interesting features of the test data as it now stands which are worth examining. Both tests have a high test re-test reliability (0·88 and 0·85), showing that there is a distinct element of consistency present.

Test B has a higher correlation with the N.F.E.R. Arithmetic Test C.1 than Test A:

	A	B
C.1	0·31	0·54

This is most likely due to the fact that Test B has a more arithmetical connotation, it requires actual computation, and in the eyes of a junior school child has more orientation to 'sums'. Test A is more game-form in its construction and involves no written computation, although a study of the sets chosen shows mental computation being undertaken by the children.

Jill chose her first set by taking a two of hearts, then an eight, a queen and a four. She next picked up an eight of spades and completed the set with an ace of diamonds. The student concerned could see no obvious connection between these cards and asked why she had collected them. The girl replied, 'I picked the two, missed out five numbers and then picked the eight. Missed out three more and then picked the queen, missed out five and took a four, etc.' This girl had counted in two different sequences and carried the sequences over and beyond the playing-card suit – quite a complicated operation. Jonathan used ratio in assembling a set and Andrew made up sums (two, three, four and five added together make fourteen – picking up an ace and a four). Many children were very inventive in selecting their sets. Gary only collected one set in the five minutes, but told a very creative story about the king and queen and their court. This highlighted a serious inadequacy of the marking system used in this inquiry, which only rewarded fluency of response. Another boy gave two reasons for every set he chose. Again the marking instructions took no account of this. It became obvious that test A produced a situation from which it was possible to gather far more than just an assessment of the number of responses. The quality of response seems to indicate that perhaps a weighted scoring system could be developed, or use could be made of some of the hypothesised primary traits of creativity, fluency, flexibility, originality, elaboration, etc., first suggested by Guilford (39) and later developed by Torrance (93). In this inquiry the use of these tests did indicate an area which could be rewarding if studied further.

Test B also produced unusual responses which could not be rewarded under the scoring system as detailed here. Many children made up sums involving length, weight, liquid measure and money. One could say this was creative use of the material, and perhaps a directive regarding this ought to have been included in the instructions. Louise was one of many children who used a system to make up her sums. She made up a sum and then used the same figures and changed the sign. For example,

$$63 + 2 = \qquad 63 \times 2 =$$
$$63 - 2 = \qquad 63 \div 2 =$$

Other high-scoring children usually utilised the combining of two figures to make up sums ($26 - 3 = 23$). Once they had discovered this principle, the number of options open to them increased, and so they both made up large numbers of sums and also, under the scoring system, were rewarded more for their efforts.

Janet, whose total score was only 22, was one of the few children to include fractions. She produced $\frac{6}{3} \times 2 = 4$ and $6 - \frac{2}{3} = 5\frac{1}{3}$. She also was the only child in the sample to set out a division sum as $2\overline{)36}^{\,18}$ the usual approach being $36 \div 2 = 18$. If originality had been assessed and defined as producing a unique response, this girl may have had a high originality rating.

On examination it can be seen that Test A has a definite spatial orientation and many children, in working the test, concentrated on card patterns and symbols. Test B, on the other hand, has a greater accent on fluency, the number of responses in this test being considerably greater than the number of sets produced in Test A. The marks on Test A ranged from 0 to 17, with a mean of 6, while on Test B, the marks ranged from 0 to 131 with a mean of 49.

Distributions of these marks for the sample are given in Tables C and D. Test B also is purely figural and involves to a great extent the re-combining of material already presented and isolated for use. In view of these differences, it is not surprising that when intercorrelated a low coefficient is obtained:

$$r_{ab} = 0.31 \ (N = 54)$$

Although both tests call for a creative use of mathematics they seem to involve different aspects of what appears to be a very wide frame of reference.

CREATIVITY AND PHYSICAL EDUCATION: AN EXPLORATORY ATTEMPT AT EVALUATION

My aim here was to try to assess creative ability in P.E., and use this assessment in a factor analysis, along with the results of other wide-ranging assessments and tests.

I had defined creativity for purposes of this inquiry as 'the complex abilities involved in reinterpreting ideas induced by a

Table C: Distribution of the sample on Test A

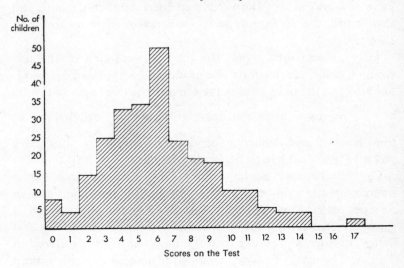

Table D: Distribution of the sample on Test B

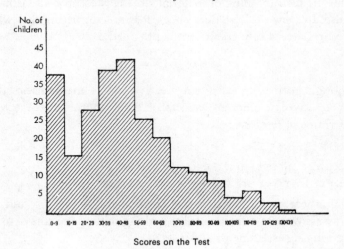

variety of given stimuli, and subsequently in innovating new ideas'. I could find no previous attempts to assess creative ability in physical education using a similar criterion, i.e. one based mainly on work inspired by Guilford and his associates at the University of Southern California. I decided therefore to begin by basing my assessments of creative ability in P.E. on some of the hypothesised primary traits of creativity suggested by Guilford (39) – namely, fluency, flexibility and originality. The children were in eleven classes in five schools, and assessments were made as part of a normal P.E. session which was taken in every case by myself. Two raters were used, myself being constant and the other rater changing as a suitable colleague was available. Raters working with me received detailed instructions on the organisation, ranking procedure and criteria for assessment (see Appendix 2).

There were three aspects to the rating in P.E.:

(*a*) working without apparatus or equipment;
(*b*) working with 'small equipment';
(*c*) working with 'large apparatus'.

Raters assessed children for fluency, flexibility and originality on each of these aspects – nine ratings in all. Children were graded first on a five-point scale. Then the three fluency grades were added, as were the grades for flexibility and originality. The children were then placed in rank order in their class for each variable. The rankings of the two raters were averaged and these averaged rankings were then standardised into sigma scores.

The following criteria for rating were used:

1 *Fluency*
High rating. The accent here is on 'many ideas'. Children rated highly will show a host of different activities. Facility in the work and speed of change would also rate highly.
Low rating. Low ratings will be given when children show few ideas. There will be repetition of one activity.

2 *Flexibility*
High rating. Children who are able to show many variations on a single theme will be rated highly. These children will vary the

E

activity easily. For example, a ball may be used in a variety of ways in quick succession, or similarly one part of the body may be used for a variety of movements or one piece of apparatus used in many ways.

Low rating. A low rating implies that the child is not able to express one basic idea or movement in a variety of ways. The same movement will be repeated and there will be little or no elaboration of this basic theme.

3   *Originality*

High rating. Children rated highly will show imagination in the use of the body, apparatus and equipment where appropriate. This will lead to work which is individual and different from others. Unique work should be rewarded, as should the originator of an idea quickly taken up by others.

Low rating. Low rating will be given where children use common activities and movements. These children will show no ability in originating new ideas, activities or movements. Their work will be characterised by copying. The poorest will add nothing individual to the ideas gleaned from others.

The instructions to the children for the first part of the assessment, using no apparatus or equipment, was as follows:

'Find a space in the hall. Make sure you have plenty of space around you.

'Without using any apparatus at all, I want you to show me as many different ways of moving your body as you can. You can either move about or stay in one place or both. Jumps, rolls, swings, turns, balances, movement on hands or any other kind of movement can be used. You can use the whole or part of your body, supporting yourself in any way you like. Let me see a variety of movements. You have about two minutes for this task. Begin.'

For the second part, using small equipment, ropes, ball, quoits, wooden blocks, bean-bags and hand-bats, etc., were available. The instructions were:

'You may pick up one or more pieces of small equipment which has been set out. Use it in any way you like. Try to make up an interesting activity which requires skill to do and which shows you have thought out good uses for the equipment. Try to do something different from the others in the class. Begin.'

Large apparatus as supplied by the L.E.A. to the school was available for Part Three, when the instructions were:

'Look at the large apparatus which has been set out. I am going to ask you to use it for activities for a total of about two minutes. During that time I want you to make up some new movements. Try to think of unusual ways of using the apparatus. Do whatever you like, providing it is not dangerous for you. You can use more than one piece of apparatus if you like. If you do this, think of a way other than walking or running to link up your work. I am interested to see a wide range of your activities and movements, not the same one repeated. Use your imagination and show me your best work. Begin.'

INTER-RATER COMPATIBILITY was established as follows: Fluency 0·72, flexibility 0·71 and originality 0·68 (N = 66). These figures indicate a broad measure of agreement between the raters in assessing the qualities. It would appear that the interpretations were similar, and, indeed, one would be suspicious of very high estimates of compatibility, as by the nature of the test situation it was not possible for both raters to see exactly the same activities at the same time, and the assumption was made that in combining the rating a more accurate all-round indication of overall performance was gained.

Very briefly the results of the factor analysis, with respect to the ratings in P.E., showed that the assessments had a small but significant loading on the general factor, named 'verbal intelligence'. This would indicate that a certain amount of verbal educational ability was required in the test situations or was rewarded by the raters. There were similar small but significant loadings of the P.E. (originality) assessment on the factor called 'Creative ability in drama', and on the factor named 'Teacher-rated creativity'. The former involved movement in a form something like charades, and so is not surprising, while the latter had verbal educational connections and echoes the first point made. Perhaps the main finding from the analysis, with respect to this section, was the existence of P.E. as a content factor of creativity. Most of the creative activities assessed, creative writing, painting, model-making, drama and P.E., appeared like this. The factorial pattern in all of them followed a similar layout. Several overtly associated variables (in this case ratings of fluency, flexibility and originality in P.E.) appeared with high loadings, along with others having significant but low loadings.

In general terms, what in fact emerged was that, although the P.E. assessments measured different attributes from the academic tests, the two sets of measures had common variance, which may have been attributable to 'g', which was reflected in the children's performances; or, to state the corollary, the P.E. assessments did measure the same qualities as intelligence tests, but in addition they reflected other qualities peculiar to this form of assessment using these criteria.

That, very briefly, was the background to the assessment, the form it took, the criteria on which it was based and the basic results which were obtained. I would like now to step back from the research and look at it tangentially against a background of the whole range of creative abilities and their relationship to the movement arts; to see creativity as one of the unifying features in the pan-disciplinary approach which will probably characterise education in the middle years of schooling.

In the research I was guided in my planning by the adage, 'From observation to action'. However unfruitful some of the work may have been, I think that this maxim proved its worth. I believe that any attempts at either provision of an environment for creative exploration in physical education or evaluation of performance will follow a pattern of observing natural activities and subsequently acting to extend these, always having quality as the keystone.

Whilst I was engaged on this study, through observation I became more and more aware of the individual. However, in this work I was purely the observer, and it became clearer than ever to me that the essential art of the P.E. teacher was not merely to observe the individual, but 'to touch that individuality'. Subsequently watching gifted teachers, I noticed that real rapport, creative progress and individual accomplishment was reached when this individuality was tapped. This was usually in a situation where there was an easy affinity between a teacher and a child, in an atmosphere again akin to the one described by Reid (75) as one of 'freedom where the teacher and the child are open to each other' Here were the fruits of the teacher's earlier astute planning; where a contrived experience provided an opportunity for judicious prompting and skilful questioning, so that the final act of creative discovery belonged to the child.

Certainly these children in the middle years of schooling relished pace, they enjoyed acquiring skills, and exercised great care and facility in selecting activities and materials. The real heights of creative endeavour were reached when this pace, skill and choice were individualised and new activities were discovered and developed anew on personal lines. I think this pattern involves cognitive and motor abilities, each engendering creative activity in the other. It provides the ongoing experiences so essential to discovery learning.

As I progressed through the experimental part of this inquiry, I was sometimes horrified by the rigidity of the stimulus, but for the sake of regularity this was unalterable. Often I saw more creative use of equipment as it was being put away than during the test session. This certainly illustrated to me the extreme need for flexibility of organisation if one were indeed to try to assess flexibility of performance.

I was also led to wonder whether the teacher needed a means of recording creative ability. This touched on one of the central dilemmas of the teacher in any informal learning situation: How to record progress. I decided that if the teacher was to structure progression and ensure sequential learning in a creative setting, record-keeping in both the creative ability and skills areas of physical education was a first requisite. Without an efficient system of recording, much discovery learning may well be labelled 'uneconomic'.

In a recent issue of the *Journal of Creative Behaviour* Hughes (50) put forward the view that 'the dominant idea of our period in history is creativity'. If we accept this – and it is certainly a fashionable notion – we need to examine whether our current practices in physical education are such that the conditions for the enhancement of creativity are present. If one of the dominant developmental needs of children in the middle years is for creative thinking, how can physical education be used as a vehicle for encouraging this? My own work has stressed recording and evaluation. But by whom? Two external raters. Davis and Miller (21) lay great stress, quite rightly I am sure, on self-evaluation, but this was completely left out of my reckoning. Self-evaluation is a common feature of much work that I have seen recently, but my experience while working on this research poses the questions: Was it followed up? Was it extended? Was it regularised by recording? Were children trained to increase their ability to evaluate their own efforts?

The experience of teachers working in vertically grouped infant classes would lead us to believe that some children do need training and encouragement in techniques of self-evaluation if they are not to become rather self-satisfied and content merely to repeat areas of success rather than extend and develop them. We would all think of instances in physical education where children have required teacher-guidance to raise a level of performance before the responsibility for further learning, evaluation and subsequent progress was accepted by the pupil.

Mackworth (62) distinguishes between two types of person – problem-solvers and problem-finders. He equates the former with convergent thinking and the latter with divergent thinking, and suggests that teachers are too involved in identifying problem-solvers, which they do well. He further suggests – and I have some supporting evidence for this – that teachers do not easily identify problem-finders. It is my view that physical education is one area of the curriculum where problem-finders can be well catered for and that the trained observer can identify such children when they are involved in physical activities. If, as Mackworth suggests, these problem-finders are creative, then physical education may well offer an area where they can be identified.

ASSESSMENT OF CREATIVE ABILITY IN DRAMA

The assessment of creative ability in drama involved collecting ratings for fluency, flexibility and originality of performance by the children. As little work had been done in this field, it was again felt that the rating should be based on Guilford's ideas about primary traits of creativity.

The ratings were obtained as part of a normal classroom activity. I devised a game-like situation which was something like 'Charades'. Children worked in small groups making up actions and mimes. They were easily identifiable to raters by a number band worn on the arm. The children had used these bands previously on several occasions to play games, so they wore them without any self-consciousness.

The complete instructions used were as follows:

Equipment to be provided

Mirrors, masks, dressing-up material, hats, tools and various types of sticks.

Instructions

Say: 'We are going to play a dressing-up, acting game. It is a game something like charades. There are only actions and movements – *no words at all*. You will only have about a minute.

'Here are some articles you may use [indicate the equipment provided]. . . You may choose any of these you like, but remember that using many articles does not always mean you do the best acting. *You* are more important than the articles you select.

'Select your articles and try to 'become' the character you represent. What would they do, how would they do it and why would they act in the way they do? You can make any actions you wish and move about just as you like! If you use material, use it imaginatively. See [demonstrate]. It can be a cloak or a skirt or a heavy bundle. If you use a mask, you can move your mouth easily: this helps you to change the face. Look at yourself in the mirror. What does it make you feel like? We are going to try to guess who you are, what you are doing and what kind of person you are [happy, sad, angry, lonely, gay, joyful, rich, poor, well-liked, or hated, young or old]. Do the things that the person you represent would do in the way they would do them. Show us the way they walk, how they feel, how they might eat a meal.

'Don't copy someone else. Do something which is different from the others – something you have made up. Show us all your good ideas. You may have an unusual use for the equipment you choose: the stick could be a tool or anything you like.

'1st Group – begin as soon as you like.'

As each group took part they were assessed by two raters, who used the following criteria in making their judgements:

Drama: assessment of children's creative ability
Guide to raters. Assessors will rate children separately on each of the three points listed below.

1   *Fluency*
High rating. Children rated highly must show many ideas in their work. The representation will be characterised by a flow of ideas. The child will show a variety of detail which could be the result of new avenues of thought opening up as the work progresses.

Low rating. A low rating will be given where the work is characterised by few ideas, lack of imagination and a stilted, stereotyped approach. These children will often wait for cues from others, need prompts and copy other behaviour.

2   *Flexibility*
High rating. Children rated highly will show an easy adaptation to the role. They should be rewarded for variation within a single idea. They may adopt a single style, emphasis or mood and will use a number of different ways or variations in presenting the particular emphasis they have adopted. (E.g. One mood . . . gloomy . . . many ways of showing this.) It is children who show a variety of ideas springing from one basic theme who will rate highly on this quality.

Low rating. A low rating will be given where there is rigidity in the work. There will be little evidence of depth of perception, ideas will not be developed and there will be no adaptive use of material. The same device will usually be adopted throughout to show whatever is in the child's mind.

3 *Originality*

High rating. A highly rated performance will be characterised by unusual, less obvious, unlikely or unexpected associations in the mime. There should be some degree of uniqueness (perhaps in the creative use of props). There may be an unusual response shown which does not involve using the equipment provided. A new situation set up by the child, involving a creative response, would rate highly, as would an individual interpretation of the materials available.

Low rating. A low rating will be given to work having much in common with other interpretations. There will be waiting, looking around and following the leads of others. The poorest will add nothing individual to the ideas of others.

In order to check on the effectiveness of the rating procedure, inter-marker compatibility was calculated. This worked out, using a stratified sample, as follows:

Fluency	0·52
Flexibility	0·57
Originality	0·49 (N=66)

It was thought that these lower-compatibility co-efficients were due to there being a more interpretive element involved in rating drama, and that each rater would see the child's work against his/her own background and training, as well as in the light of the given criteria. However, it was conceded that, using a sample selected without regard to the use of different raters, it was not possible to tell if one rater was extremely suspect. To investigate this, the rating of each of the four raters used was correlated with my rating, which was constant throughout. The results of this analysis are set out below:

Rater	N	Fluency	Flexibility	Originality
1	65	0·47	0·42	0·73
2	75	0·51	0·46	0·57
3	106	0·58	0·47	0·67
4	67	0·59	0·61	0·59

The similarity of the coefficients between raters and those obtained using the stratified sample would seem to support the inference that with this sample and these raters, although there was some measure of agreement between the raters, either they were rating different aspects of the qualities under review, or their interpretation of the performances differed. The combination of the ratings would contribute to a more comprehensive assessment.

The drama ratings appeared in the factor analysis in much the same way as the P.E. ratings already discussed. One interesting point was that the peer rating of conformity (acquired by asking children to name anyone in their class who never got into any kind of trouble) was associated with the factor of creative ability in drama. In the eyes of other children, the fact that children have to become submissive and accepting towards the form of material is interpreted as conformity. It also highlights the fact that creative ability in drama does involve a disciplined response to the medium, and not unrestrained licence, which would not be rated highly under the criteria set out for this study. It is, indeed, one of the central themes developed by Bohm (7a). He concludes: 'What is really needed to create . . . is the state of mind that is continually and increasingly observant of the fact of the actual order of the medium in which one is working.'

In all the creative activities rated there was a 'halo' effect. Correlations between fluency, flexibility and originality ratings was about 0·8 in P.E., painting, models, creative writing and drama. It seems difficult for raters to differentiate between these three aspects when judging creative ability in a school activity. There is a 'totality' judgement reflected in all three assessments. This is the overall impression made on the rater by either the performance or the product.

The attempt to assess creative ability in drama, although not really productive in terms of experimental research, did provide a situation where children with the ability to reinterpret ideas, express emotion and use movement to reveal imaginative thought could be easily identified even if their work would not be so easily quantified. It is in these more general terms that the work may be useful to teachers.

ASSESSMENT OF CREATIVE WRITING

Many attempts have been made to develop objective approaches to assessing creative writing. Lawton (57) describes an attempt to quantify children's writing in a very objective way which is typical of many similar approaches. These have involved counting adjectives, use of subordinate clauses and so on. I decided to adopt a rating technique based on assessing fluency, flexibility and originality again. The evidence regarding the reliability of teacher ratings has been discussed in Chapter 1. I tried to increase the efficiency of the rating on the lines suggested by research evidence by providing the raters with criteria to guide them as follows:

Guide to raters:
General
Assessors will rate children separately on each of the three points listed below.

1 *Fluency*
High rating. Scripts rated highly on this variable will contain *many* ideas. The accent here is on a profusion of ideas without regard to quality.
Low rating. A low rating will be given to scripts showing few ideas.

2 *Flexibility*
High rating. Highly rated scripts should show a wide range of reference, a width of ideas related to any particular topic and a number of developments on a single theme. Different ways of describing the same thing would also contribute to a high rating.
Low rating. A low rating will be given to scripts showing a single, stereotyped, rigid approach with little development of such themes as are used.

3 *Originality*
High rating. A highly rated script should show an element of uniqueness of response, an unusual or arresting choice and treatment of subject-matter, and evidence of a creative approach involving creative thinking. Any individual organisation of the

work, style of writing or sense of humour should also be rewarded.

Low rating. Poor scripts will show little or no individuality of approach or content. These scripts will contain such stereotyped forms as 'Once upon a time . . .' and '. . . they lived happily ever after'.

Children were asked to write an interesting story on one topic. Ten titles were given which suggested the unusual. Some of these titles have been used previously by other investigators, whilst others were used for the first time by me.

The instructions and titles were as follows:

Instructions

We would like you to write the most interesting and exciting story you can think of about *one* of the topics listed below. There is no time-limit, but we think it will take you about twenty minutes. Try to write clearly, but do not worry too much about your writing, spelling, etc. Instead, try to put into your story as many good ideas as you can. Choose any one of the following topics or make up a similar one of your own:

1 The dog that doesn't bark.
2 The woman who can but won't talk.
3 The cock that doesn't crow.
4 The girl who wants to be a good footballer.
5 The boy who wants to be a nurse.
6 The horse that won't run.
7 Miss Jones stopped teaching . . .
8 The lion that won't roar.
9 The cat who could only run backwards.
10 The 'fridge that ate the food.'

Creative writing appeared in the factor analysis in the same way as the other creative abilities already discussed. Although creative writing was called a 'creative ability' factor, it must be recognised that a considerable verbal educational influence enters into it, as the rated response was written material. The relationship between the creative writing variables and English attainment is illustrated when one looks at the correlations between these measures.

Correlations of creative writing and English attainment variables

		English attainment		
		N.F.E.R. D.2	Eng. Test 2	Eng. Test 3*
Creative writing	Fluency	0·526	0·475	0·460
	Flexibility	0·555	0·497	0·491
	Originality	0·497	0·466	0·431

There were moderately high correlations between the creative writing variables and English attainment tests. However, the converse is also true that correlations basically in the region of 0·5 show that the raters did assess qualities not reflected in the formal English attainment tests. This last point is of real relevance to teachers. It is possible for children with limited verbal educational ability to show that they can express ideas imaginatively in written form, providing the criteria for assessment are not heavily weighted on spelling, punctuation, etc. It is not suggested that these things are unimportant, but that they may be more easily acquired if children have experienced some success in presenting their own ideas in written form and have had their efforts praised. In this way they see the need for correct use of language conventions, and soon accept the discipline of learning them, approaching the task in a more positive way.

The choice of title for the creative writing produced an unusual result. The titles are set out below with the number of children who selected each one.

---

* All three English tests covered the range of English achievement usually associated with children, aged 9 to 11 years, who formed this sample. All the tests contained comprehension, word study, sentence construction and patterning, and spelling. N.F.E.R. Test D.2. is published; English Tests 2 and 3 were constructed for local authority use in selection and grading and are not published.

The dog that doesn't bark 22
The woman who can but won't talk . . 9
The cock that doesn't crow . . . 14
The girl who wants to be a good footballer . 26
The boy who wants to be a nurse . . 11
The horse that won't run 19
Miss Jones stopped teaching 14
The lion that won't roar 14
The cat who could only run backwards . 23
The 'fridge that ate the food . . . 101
A different title made up 12

Total 265

The distribution is fairly well spread, with the exception of the title 'The 'fridge that ate the food'. This seemed to catch the imagination of the children in a startling manner. It is the only title which is completely domestic, and this may be one reason why it was chosen. The other two with domestic connections concern the cat and the dog. These were also popular choices. There is support here for the idea that successful stimuli for children in the 8–13 age-range will usually be based on direct experience, and yet capable of imaginative interpretation. Twelve children made up their own titles: as the number who did this was small, in terms of the criteria, this merited a high grading for originality. In fact, children who made up a title usually produced an imaginative essay. Some children used the ideas given but changed the title slightly. This produced such titles as 'the gobbling 'fridge', 'Mrs Richardson stopped teaching' and 'The horse that never won'. The unusual element in most of the titles sparked off a similar line of thought for Marie, whose title was 'The mouse who would not steal cheese'. Three boys deviated completely from the ideas given and produced these titles: 'The diddyland monster', 'Men in space', and 'The boy from outer-space'.

David, aged 9 years, a boy of limited verbal ability, with an I.Q. of 104 on the N.F.E.R. P.V.2 Test, was the only child in the sample to illustrate his work. His essay shows real originality of story, a very unusual basic idea, and an indication that he can use his creative thinking to good purpose. The version given here is corrected, as the original left much to be desired in the way of spelling and punctuation, etc.

The diddyland monster

In Kennoularey ten years ago there was a certain wizard who turned all the diddy people into mini-diddy people. This was quite a change as they went 1/32 of an inch smaller. This may not seem much to you but when you are only 3/32 of an inch high it's quite a lot.

But this has nothing to do with the story really, except that the wizard was turned into a giant 1 7/8 inches high. Soon the mini-diddy people formed an army of mini-diddy resistance men and they tried every form of trick to capture the wizard. The wizard was too clever for them. He had magic on his side. One day a bright chap said, 'If we lassoo him we could pull him into a trap. See, I'll draw you a picture.' [That was the illustration referred to above.] The plan worked, but not without lots of other adventures. There is no time to tell these here. There is only time to say that the wizard was killed.

The use of new words like 'diddy' and 'mini' associated with the mass media shows the effect that these factors have on young children. David had average scores on English attainment tests, but had some mathematical flair, scoring highly on both arithmetic attainment tests and tests of the creative use of mathematics. This ability is illustrated by the ingenious use of fractions in the story, and is also an illustration of the way in which young children naturally link their language and mathematical experiences.

The essays included here are typical of the more creative responses. They show something of the liveliness of children's writing at this stage. They are natural, full of spontaneous, easy use of language, and characterised by imaginative ideas. They were written quickly and without preparation, but in some cases they do show the effects of structured approaches to language teaching, whilst they still retain the creative flow associated with the written work of children at this age. Teachers will recognise in them the quality they see in work from their own classes where a stimulus has been particularly successful in providing the children with a thinking situation.

VIVIENNE

Mr Knowlson stopped teaching

Mr Knowlson stopped teaching. . . . 'Who did that?' he said. A large noise had been made. A whirring, buzzing sound. None of the children had done it, he knew, for it was too loud for a human to make. He looked out of the window. There, sitting on a bench, was a middle-aged woman. 'What are you doing there?' he said. She pointed a finger. It had a long green nail about 7 inches long. 'None of your business.' She grabbed a child and poked her with one of her nails. At once she seemed to be in a trance. She obeyed everything the woman said. One by one, the woman injected each of the children and each child reacted in the same way. Mr Knowlson said, 'Stop. You cannot do this to my class. I will send the . . .' 'Grab him, make him prisoner.' All the children from about the age of eleven and twelve bound their teacher around the feet and hands. The woman took off a wig and mask and appeared to be the most ugly creature on earth. Her hair was raven black, her face was dotted with pimples and warts, her nose was as long as her hand from the wrist to the tips of her nails. 'Have you heard of witches?' she said. 'No,' said Mr Knowlson bluntly. 'Bah,' she said. 'Well, I'm one, see!' She pointed at one book and changed it into a frog. Mr Knowlson remembered the story of 'Puss in Boots'. 'Huh,' he said. 'I bet you could not change my children back and fly away for ever.' The boasting witch did this and they carried on the lesson. The Headmaster came in. 'I was sure I heard a noise in here. What has happened?' 'Nothing,' said Mr Knowlson, sniggering as he saw the frog jump across the floor.

SHEREE

The cat who could only run backwards

A long, long time ago there was a cat who walked and lived all alone in the world. One day when he was running up the lane, he became thirsty and wanted to drink so he went over the bank to the stream. When he was drinking an old lady hobbled up to him and said, 'Pussy, pussy, will you fill my pail?' The cat stared and said, 'I will not.' The old woman turned to go and the cat said, 'And don't ever bother me again.' He didn't know that this old lady was a witch. She was always kind though, and never hurt anybody unless they hurt her. If they did anything wrong she would curse them. Now, as you know the cat had done something wrong to deserve punishment, so he got it. The old lady put a curse on him that when he was older he would walk backwards wherever he went and she thought to herself, 'The people will laugh at that.' Years went by. Two years had past in fact and the cat was in the street when he started to run backwards. When he tried to run forwards he couldn't. He tried to run sideways but he couldn't do that either. All he could do was run backwards all the time. The cat thought back and remembered he didn't give the lady a drink of water by the stream. He thought that the lady would be at the stream so he raced off (backwards, of course) to the stream where he'd met the old lady before. Sure enough she was there and he said, 'I'll give you a drink of water if you uncast my spell.' So in the end she uncast the spell and the cat could run forwards. But where he lived was poor, so he went to live in the witches' house in the snug and warm. From now on the cat gets more food and all he wants. Since then witches have always had cats, so watch out on Hallo'een.

JOHN

The boy from outer-space

Mr Black stopped teaching and looked down on Charlie. He said, 'What are you doing fidgeting up your jumper. What have you got there?' Charlie showed Mister Black a queer-looking animal about the size of an orange. It had huge bulging eyes and a very long tail. Its fingers were long with suction tips and they were very wrinkled. 'Where did you get this, boy?' said Mr Black, in a very disagreeable tone. 'I got it from a strange coloured boy, who came into my back garden by space ship,' stammered Charlie. Of course Mister Black did not believe him and sent him out of the room, to get rid of this unusual animal.

When Mr Black got home that night, he found a weirdly dressed small man sitting down in the lounge. He demanded to know why he was there. The small man replied and told Mister Black that he had come from the planet Sasubo about 1,111,111,000,001,112,326,987,986 miles away. And then he raised his hand and disappeared. Mr Black was dumbfounded. Suddenly he heard a dead voice say, 'Why-did-you-tell-Charlie-off?' Of course, Mister Black was terrified and ran out of the house.

In the morning Mr Black begged Charlie to bring the strange animal to school. Charlie was very surprised and nearly fainted.

F

BEVERLEY

The girl who wants to be a good footballer

Jenny was not an abnormal girl but one thing made her peculiar, she wanted to be a footballer.

She had loved football when she was a small girl and often went to football matches with her father. Later in life, she played with some boys at football and they said she was quite good. Her mother thought it was just a childish phase and would soon pass but it didn't.

By this time she was 15 and still loved football. She wanted to be a footballer but her mother said it was ridiculous and she was silly. One time she pleaded with her headmistress to take up football but her headmistress said it was very unlady-like and refused. Jenny was taken to a psychiatrist and although he tried, he could not find out why she liked it so much.

Jenny was ready to leave school. She became a secretary to a business man and in her spare time she would go to the playing fields near her home and played football.

Then her big chance came. Advertised in the local newspaper was an ad. for a secretary in a football ground. Her parents were not keen on her applying for this job because she only got half the salary of her other job, but in spite of this, she applied and was given the job. Her first day went well and afterwards she asked her boss if she could play football on the pitch. He agreed and after that coached her every night until she was a good player.

One day he said he had a surprise for her and took her to see a man he knew. The man played football with her and afterwards said, 'I am President of the W.F.C. (The Women's Football Club) and I would like to hire you.'

Jenny was thrilled. She went home and told her mother her news. After a bit of persuasion her mother let her accept and she went to the football club. She grew to be a very famous footballer and often played for England's Women's team.

She was very pleased. After all her hard work to become a footballer, she had finally made it. I think her mother was pleased too, although she did not show it.

CHARLES

The dog that doesn't bark

There was once a man who bought a dog for his son's birthday. The dog was a mongrel called Duke.

The boy went for a holiday to the seaside. The boy and the dog went along a cliff-top walk. They stood on the cliff – looked at the jagged rocks below and then looked out to sea. Meanwhile another dog was walking along the path a bit further along and when he saw Duke he let out a terrifying bark. This scared the boy so much that he lost his balance and fell over the cliff. The boy died on contact with the rocks. From then on, the dog was never to bark again.

The boy's father thought the dog had pushed him over so he gave the dog to the dog's home. Because it had been wrongly accused, the dog escaped, never to be seen by humans again. Whether the dog returned to the same deadly spot again I do not know, but a dog very much like it was found dead on the same rocks.

HELEN

The cock that doesn't crow

Farmer Jones had ten big cocks but only one cock awoke him and the village people. The one that awoke them was called Crower. Every morning the whole village awoke when Crower started to crow. Everybody and thing in the village were very grateful that Crower had such a loud voice except for a farmer named Jake.

Farmer Jake had always hated Farmer Jones and anything that belonged to him because most people bought things from Farmer Jones' farm, for Jake was so mean.

One day Jake had an idea. If he stopped Crower from crowing everybody in the village would be angry with Crower and Farmer Jones.

That night Jake crept to the hen coop where Crower slept and put a bag over Crower's head so that he wouldn't know when it was sunrise.

When Crower woke up the next morning it was sunrise but Crower didn't know it was sunrise because he had a bag over his head and it was still dark to him.

The first person to wake in the village was Robert the horse-breeder; he had to go round the village waking everybody up.

There was such a commotion. The horses neighed, the cows bellowed, for it was well over milking time. Everyone in the village marched over to Farmer Jones's farm and told him what had happened and they had decided to cut off Crower's head.

Sadly, Farmer Jones went to fetch Crower. Suddenly he came hurrying back with Crower with the bag over his head. 'Look!' he exclaimed, 'one of Farmer Jake's bags on his head. Farmer Jake must have put this on to stop him from waking us up.'

In the end Jake got his head chopped off.

JILL

The lion that wouldn't roar

Tom Grim was the owner of Grim's Circus. He was travelling to Hull. They arrived in the afternoon after they had spent a week travelling. After putting the tents up Jimmy Green went to feed Royal, the Circus lion. The trouble with Royal was he had never roared in his life, so when anybody came he was too frightened to scare them away with a roar. Jimmy was the one who cleaned his cage, fed him and cared for him when he was ill. That night while everybody was watching the show Royal crept out of his cage, because Jimmy forgot to close it properly. His pads made no noise as he walked out of the field into the town. Royal never roared (as I have told you) so that the people wouldn't know he was there.

The show had finished and Jimmy Green went to Royal's cage to say 'Good night', but when he saw the cage was empty he dashed to Mr Grim and shouted 'Royal's cage is empty.' 'What?' he said, and Jimmy had to tell it all again. Immediately after he told it to Mr Grim, Mr Grim got nets, forks and men. Meanwhile Royal had gone in Mr Hill's house. Luckily the family was coming from the show. John, Mr Hill's son had two pet mice, one called Dixie and one called Pixie. Royal went upstairs where the mice were kept, but when Royal saw the mice he was so frightened that he gave an enormous roar! It was so loud that the two mice ran into their beds which were made of straw and lay there trembling. The men heard it and ran to where the roar came from. They found him and put a net over him. The only thing was that nobody knew what made him roar!

KAREN

The 'fridge that ate the food

'I,' said the 'fridge, 'do not see why human beings should eat all the food, whilst we 'fridges have to starve.' 'Well, we are tired of hearing you complaining, so shut up,' said the cooker angrily. 'All right then,' replied the 'fridge. 'I shall do something which all of you dare not do.' 'What,' shouted the cooker, the cupboards and the other kitchen furniture. 'I'm not going to tell you,' said the 'fridge indignantly, 'so be quiet.' 'All right then, don't tell us what you are going to do,' replied the cooker.

The next day at breakfast, Mrs Warber went into the kitchen to make the breakfast for her two children and her husband. 'Where's the bacon and eggs I bought yesterday?' said Mrs Warber. 'I'm sure I put them in the 'fridge when I came home from the shops.' 'We haven't taken them,' shouted the children. 'Daddy must have done.' 'Dear me, I will go and ask him,' said Mrs Warber. As soon as she had left the kitchen, the 'fridge cried out, 'Ha, Ha, Ha, she will never know that I ate them.' 'You ate them,' shouted the kitchen furniture all at once. 'Yes,' replied the 'fridge. 'But it's stealing,' said the cooker. 'Well,' replied the 'fridge, 'what if it is stealing, I can't be told off or even found out.'

Three days later after the 'fridge had eaten some salad *and* the container it was in, the 'fridge was feeling sick. 'Ooh, ooh,' said the 'fridge. 'I feel so sick.' 'Serves you right,' answered the cooker. The other kitchen furniture had no sympathy with Freddy (this was the 'fridge's name) at all. After that Freddy never ate any more food. He had learned his lesson.

ASSESSMENT OF CREATIVE ABILITY IN MODEL-MAKING

Following the pattern of the assessment of creative abilities in various areas of the curriculum already detailed, three aspects of creative ability in model-making were rated – namely, fluency, flexibility and originality.

Specific instructions for the assessments were given as follows:

Instructions

Say: 'Today I would like you to make a model. There are lots of materials here you can use. There are some items you will not have used in model-making before. This does not matter. It will only make the construction more interesting for you.

'I want you to look carefully at the material. Notice the different shapes. Think about them. Do they suggest anything to you? Some may suggest animals; others may look like a head; others may remind you of buildings or chimneys or trees or people or birds or fishes. There are many other things which the materials here may suggest to you. Try to make an unusual model. See if you can find a very unusual use for some of the things you see. Use your own ideas. Do not copy other models you see. There are no right and wrong models. I would like to see the best model you can make using your own imagination.'

N.B. – As the teacher reads the instruction, appropriate pieces of the material available can be indicated as the list is read, e.g. apple as the word 'head' is read; corks as the word 'chimneys' is read; potato as the word 'animals' is read.

List of materials to be available
1. Assorted buttons. 2. Assorted feathers. 3. Wire. 4. Wooden cocktail sticks. 5. Cup-hooks. 6. Glue. 7. Paste. 8. Assorted corks. 9. Fruit and vegetables in season. 10. Samples of cloth. 11. Variety of nails. 12. Card. 13. Paints. 14. Sellotape. 15. Pebbles.

Raters were given a full indication of qualities which would be rated high and low for each variable in the following guide to raters.

Guide to raters:
1 *Fluency*
High rating. Highly rated models will contain many different materials. These materials will have been used to produce a number of new effects. Many different ideas expressed in one model should be rewarded. The accent here is on 'many' ideas and uses.

Low rating. A low rating will be given to models using few materials, few constructional ideas and producing an overall effect of immaturity.

2 *Flexibility*

High rating. Highly rated models should show a variety of uses for the same material, e.g. (*a*) many ideas for joining material, (*b*) buttons used for wheels, faces, as a body, etc., (*c*) any given object used for several distinct purposes.

A breadth of ideas concerned with one aspect of the model would also earn a high rating, e.g. (*a*) a profusion of ideas on pattern. (*b*) use of the same material to produce different effects.

The model itself may have the quality of suggesting further ideas which could be developed.

Low rating. Models rated poorly will show a very limited range of ideas and uses of materials. There will be little elaboration or development of those which are presented.

3 *Originality*

High rating. A high rating will be given to models which are unlike others in idea, representation, use of materials or treatment of a theme. Any aspect which has an element of uniqueness when compared with other models will earn a high assessment.

Low rating. These models will be characterised by a monotonous sameness. The product will show that there has been no attempt to think creatively about the task or to give an individual interpretation of the medium.

Inter-rater compatibility was assessed as shown below.

Model-making

	Inter-rater compatibility
Fluency	0·68
Flexibility	0·66
Originality	0·62 (N = 66)

These coefficients indicated a considerable degree of similarity between the two raters, but an interpretive element must inevitably enter the rating of a creative product, such as a model which makes use of unusual materials. It is inferred that different aspects of the creative use of the media are seen by the two raters, and that a better overall assessment is gained by combining the ratings.

In various try-out attempts for this assessment, it was evident that if a creative use of media and an imaginative response was to be elicited it was essential to provide a wide range of materials. There had to be sufficient articles to allow an easy choice, and to present children with a situation which gave them an opportunity to decide on an individual course of action. This is seen in most school classrooms. The most imaginative responses emanate from sources which allow children to use materials in a personal way. In these circumstances they are presented with a problem which suggests a response which is really their own, not copied from another child; although the creative child often builds imaginatively on to an idea initiated elsewhere.

The models produced were in no way stereotyped. The examples given in the introduction did not inhibit the children. They certainly acted as a guide for less creative children, who often thought no further than the ideas given. However, many children looked at the material and began to make unusual models immediately, while others waited, looked around, thought and generally let their ideas crystallise before commencement. This period of latency for some children seemed an essential part of their approach, and was noticed in every different class. The most persistent comment recorded by observers was that ideas of real creative quality seemed to come to children when they picked up an object, handled it and turned it around and over. This physical contact seemed to produce the ability to see the object in a new light, as part of a new design, or in an unusual setting. Often they seemed to take a second look which gave a fresh insight into the possibilities for original use of the object. All the ideas noted here are present whenever children are observed taking decisions about model-making with 'junk materials'. In a teaching as distinct from an experimental situation it is usually the teacher who helps the child 'to take a second look' before leaving the final act of creative discovery and fulfilment to the child.

Often models which were made were small: this was obviously influenced by the type of material presented. Observers commented on this and a small study was made to look at the educational possibilities of large-scale models.

THE VALUE OF LARGE-SCALE MODELS

The construction of large-scale models in schools is becoming more and more commonplace. As one visits schools, delighted children are eager to show their guests a bewildering array of rockets, astronauts, totem poles, dinosaurs, windmills, dragons and the like. The evident enthusiasm and enjoyment displayed by children who have been involved in making these models, usually considerably larger than their creators, led us to consider, in some detail, the intrinsic value that this constructional activity seemed to have for children. As ideas began to flow, it became obvious that the worth of this work could be evaluated under three main headings: developmental, psychological and practical. Naturally there were some difficulties of classification, and some ideas seemed to belong in more than one category, but a fuller appreciation of the appeal of the large model emerged, for all those taking part in the discussion, as the notions took shape under these three headings.

Perhaps the most obvious values noted under the developmental heading were social. An example was given of children in an infant class making a train from paper tower boxes; this became literally a vehicle for role-playing, a means of learning new roles, and a focus for rich conversation involving questions, description, clarification and repetition of phrases. So language development featured in all the social situations. Again, from an infant class in a deprived area came the illustration of making a series of large animal models. These included Paddington Bear, animals from *The Wind in the Willows* and some T.V. favourites. The construction of these was extremely primitive, but the teacher had cut out a section to enable children to stand inside. The anonymity of this gave less gifted children the impetus to discuss their activities, as the animal character, with other children. The probing, pertinent questions from the teacher helped this along, and presented further stimulus for thought. Through this questioning the teacher was able to help the children build up their descriptive powers, deduce meaning from the children's messages as animals, and compare the different contributions from children.

Conceptual development seemed to be aided as children saw pictures in a new light when the model developed in three dimensions. A further realisation of the relationships between the picture and the model helped clarification of the concept, particularly in the case of the dress of Queen Elizabeth, who was being modelled from a picture by 8-year-olds.

The aesthetic values of large models were especially noted under the developmental heading also. Form, order, a sense of unity, quality and a heightened awareness of shape and varying strengths of different materials were seen in many observations, but particularly in a fourth-year junior class who had built a replica of the church pipe organ. This was built with the pipes cut to scale and a record of organ music played on a portable record-player concealed inside. The aesthetic awareness seen in the selection of different materials chosen for effect, the appeal to many senses in making these choices, and the fascination which the model held for the children, encouraging them to 'take a second look', all seemed to help qualities of discrimination.

We were reminded that in a reception class children had played out their fears by using large models, which for them had intense realism. They touched them, hugged them, talked about them and included them in their play activities.

Physical development figured large in our discussions, and the importance of large models in providing many tasks of differing complexity, to assist co-ordination, was mentioned. The sheer physical manipulation of large, bulky components, which, although easily put together, posed new problems of a physical character, was often seen in work reported. When infants had to deal with these mammoth boxes, etc., the situation seemed to be strikingly productive in the field of language. The teacher, working alongside the children, was able to raise the level of their communication, not only by expanding their own speech, but also by commenting on it in such a way that new thoughts were needed to provide further answers.

Psychological values centred at first on advantages of providing concrete bases for exercises in co-operation and involvement. Levels of involvement seemed to be very high as children became absorbed in their tasks, and numerous examples were given which showed children raising levels of aspiration as their interest increased.

Sheer pleasure in the task was noted in some reports, and the fact that pleasurable activities often led to requests to repeat the procedure seemed significant.

The adoption by children of widening frames of reference was seen in a mixed group of 9-year-olds. Clive and Eric were having difficulty putting the roof on their 'gingerbread house' because of sheer weight and size. Karl, coming fresh to the problem, told them, 'You'll have to think big.'

Experimentation with alternative materials gave rise to much creative thinking, and imaginative ideas seemed to proliferate when suggestions were asked for in trying to fix the mainmast to a model of the *Golden Hind*. For children at the junior stage actually to be able to see the results of their creative thinking in concrete form seemed to be a great encouragement to further efforts. The compelling visual impact of the finished model usually provoked telling comment.

Building large models seems to provide many situations where it is easy for the teacher to arrange for less able children to become successful. This was illustrated when 8-year-olds built a coal-mine (complete with model canary) in a spare classroom by using the space under some tables. Another feature of this work was the advantage, for these children, of actually working *in* the mine, dragging the trucks in and the coal out, playing out dramatic rescue operations and talking to the 'surface' through a speaking tube. Similarly, the rockets of today do need to be built to accommodate a crew of three, and a built-in 'communication system' of the speaking-tube type needs to be there so that links with the ground controller can be established!

The practical values of large models seem to be implicit in the other two sections. However, specific practical points were further highlighted.

The model as a focal point in the classroom was frequently mentioned. There seemed to be a fascination for third-year juniors with the model of Gulliver, laid out in the middle of the room, a straw-filled torso on whom climbed hundreds of Lilliputians, complete with ladders and ropes. The impetus created by this work being carried on into the fields of literature, creative writing and drama. Sir Francis Drake, a magnificent model, 5 ft high and elaborately dressed in doublet and hose, created far more impact for 9-year-olds when he was placed in a position where children could walk all round than when he was put in a corner of the classroom.

Perhaps the most basic practical value of the model for the teacher is its use as an integrating link for a whole theme. Indeed, the model may well become the central point of work which can occupy a class for several weeks, which was the case with some of the examples given here.

Teachers who have discussed their successes using large models have mentioned a novelty value, but have also drawn attention to the necessity to pace novelty with complexity. As the model progressed in the latter, the former was renewed.

The practical uses of models for mathematical purposes are endless. The opportunities for drawing to scale, estimation, comparison and acquiring spatial concepts through looking at specific relationships in a concrete form were seen clearly in the building of the _Q.E._ II and the _Great Eastern_. This was carried out in a top junior class in a school in a very privileged area, containing a great many highly gifted children. The scheme posed difficult problems in both the mathematical and constructional field which acted as a provocative challenge to children who frequently found their tasks in school too easy. At the same time there were many other tasks available, suitable for less academically gifted children. The same class found the making of a sand yacht presented similar possibilities.

In summary, it seemed that where large models had been carefully used, with adequate planning, and where there had been careful preparation of allied activities, the stimulus provided had not only been worthwhile for its own sake, but had generated a whole series of other themes which had been successfully used as growth points for children's further inquiries.

ASSESSMENT OF CREATIVE ABILITY IN PAINTING

The general rating procedure for this assessment followed the lines previously outlined, and involved obtaining a rating for fluency, flexibility and originality.

A prepared tape was played to the children. This consisted of sound capable of varied interpretations. Some sounds were electronic, and all had an abstract quality which could lead to individual interpretations.

The actual instructions given to the children were:

Instructions

Say: 'I am going to play some music for you. Listen to it very carefully. If you close your eyes it may help you to concentrate. What does the music suggest to you? Listen very hard and forget about everything except the music. If the music suggests several different things to you, paint the one which interests you most. Try to paint the picture you think no one else will paint, a picture with lots of ideas, using the paper and paints really well, a painting which shows what *you* want to say. Try to see the picture the music brings into your mind. Remember this as well as you can, as I want you to draw this picture afterwards. You can make any notes or drawings you like to help you either during the music or immediately afterwards.

'When you have finished your painting, I would like you to give it an interesting title. Perhaps you can be thinking about this as you go along. Put your name, class and title on the back of the paper.

'Listen to the music now.'

Equipment required: Tape-recorder, $3\frac{3}{4}$ in. per sec.

In try-out it was found advantageous to repeat the playing of the tape and the instructions. As with the instructions in all the other assessments, there were suggestions which hinted at the production of many and varied ideas, and also at producing something different from the other children. These were the qualities which would eventually be rated highly, using these criteria.

The following guide was given to raters to assist them:

Guide to raters:

General

Assessors will rate children's paintings separately on each of the three variables listed below.

1   *Fluency*

High rating. Paintings given a high rating will show many ideas in the use of the material and the interpretation of the stimulus. There will be effective use of space and evidence of the flow and movement usually associated with children's paintings. There should be many techniques used and a striking result in the attempt to transfer thought from an auditory stimulus to a visual response.

Low rating. Paintings given a low rating will have a limited use of materials, few ideas in the presentation, little flow or spontaneity and show rigidity of expression.

2   *Flexibility*

High rating. There should be an emphasis on a variety of ideas used to express a central theme or themes. This may be manifested either through the treatment of the subject-matter or in the way in which material is used. The product itself may have the quality of eliciting new ideas and avenues of thought in the onlooker.

Low rating. Paintings in this category will show little imaginative use of either ideas or materials. There will be little development of colour, texture, composition or interpretation. The total effect will be formality; an unwillingness to leave the conventional or elaborate on a basic theme.

3   *Originality*

High rating. Paintings rated highly will show unusual ideas and a personal interpretation of the stimulus not found in other products. There should be some personal expression of thoughts, emotions or ideas. There may be an element of ambiguity (e.g. a lack of definition) which leads to an individual interpretation in the onlooker.

Low rating. These ratings will be illustrating an obvious response to the stimulus. They will have much in common with other paintings and be characterised by the lack of lustre associated with products produced by children from a restricted environment.

Inter-rater compatibility was established for the rating of paintings as shown in the table below.

Painting	
Inter-rater compatibility	
Fluency	0·54
Flexibility . . .	0·61
Originality . .	0·43 (N = 66)

These figures suggest that, although some agreement between raters was evident, there was also considerable divergence of opinion on some paintings. This could have been due to lack of marker sophistication at rating paintings along set criteria. It may have been caused by the second rater not following the given instructions exactly enough, but interpreting the paintings by using his own intuitive professional standards. It is quite possible for raters to arrive at different gradings and yet still be rating aspects of the same variable when asked to judge a painting which must elicit an individual response in the onlooker in the first instance. The inference is again made that combining the two ratings gives a better all-round assessment.

The paintings produced by this form of assessment were very varied, both in interpretation and technique. Many were concerned with space. This was presumably suggested by the electronic quality of some of the sounds on the tape. Even so, within the space theme there was considerable variation involving space-ships, rockets, imaginary space-creatures, moon landscapes, galaxies of stars and satellites. Another popular theme was 'an underwater world'. This may have been suggested by the rather eerie quality of some sounds on the tape. Again, there was wide variation within the theme involving fishes, imaginary sea-creatures, rich colourings, shells, coral, seaweed, mermaids, sunken wrecks, divers, skin-divers, submarines and plants. A group of children drew pictures which included trains. Some sounds were reminiscent of steam trains, which would account for this response. However, the type of train drawn varied enormously, and included ancient engines, modern diesels, miniature engines, Heath-Robinson trains and even a ghost-train. Although many children chose these themes, the abstract nature of the stimulus did produce a varied response within the basic common ideas. This kind of result must surely be the aim of a teacher when introducing stimuli to children in the hope of producing creative responses.

There were many individual interpretations which would be impossible to explain. Presumably some sound had sparked off an individual thought which the child wished to express. One boy drew a boat-race, another a screen which simply said 'The end' on it, whilst another drew a workshop showing a man sawing wood. One girl drew two children dancing in the wood, another a child playing the piano, and a third drew a man repairing a car.

A pleasing feature of the paintings was the way in which ideas from outside the main field of the idea had been used. Children had seen a relevance and used an unusual idea. Karl, aged 11 years, had obviously seen the wealth of 'space paintings' around him. He had drawn a motor-cyclist, but had equipped him, not with traditional clothes, but complete space-suit, aerials and all.

The children were asked to give their paintings a title. Many expressed imaginative ideas, making comments rather than providing formal titles. Using Torrance's (93) criteria, these would rate very highly. Examples of this were: 'Who said there was an invasion?' 'This may lead you to nowhere' and 'What was here before man?' These responses made a comment beyond anything which could be seen in the picture. I was surprised how many children spontaneously wrote on their own drawings. Sometimes this seemed to be done as an explanation; sometimes to heighten awareness of a section of the painting, or to draw attention to a particular idea which had been included. 'Balloons' were used to indicate speech, as might have been expected, but the deliberate commenting on the actual painting was something which I had not met before. Could the exhortation to originality have produced this?

When a painting has been produced, there seems to be a need in most children during the middle years of schooling to have the work appraised. Many observers commented on this fact. Children did want an opinion on their work, and they wanted this immediately, not at some time in the future. For them this is a genuine continuation of the creative act. Neither were they satisfied at this age with a casual 'Well done', which would have been accepted by younger children. They required a more balanced opinion. Certainly, some teachers are adept at providing an effective on-the-spot appraisal. It does seem a necessary ability for the teacher to acquire.

The assessment of creative ability in painting was certainly enjoyed. Playing the tape produced spontaneous language, easy laughter and a genuine desire to begin. A creative situation arose from the stimulus which also produced 'original' ideas which had their beginnings in the taped sounds. This assessment seemed to illustrate the point made by Vinacke (103) when he linked creative acts and problem-solving. He said: 'A creative situation resembles a problem situation as soon as the effort commences to achieve the final product or to convert the feelings, images, plots, etc., into a tangible medium.' I have always maintained that for the teacher arranging for really creative responses was synonymous with arranging for children to solve problems. In fact, all the attempts to assess creative ability described here can be designated 'problem-solving situations'.

SUMMARY

Some of the underlying aims which govern the content of the curriculum are presented and evaluated. The more objective approaches to curriculum, as seen in the Curriculum Development movement, are set out and used in an attempt to present a background to endeavours to evaluate creative abilities.

Discussion centres around whether creative potential in children can be identified by the teacher. Some tentative rating procedures and ideas for assessment are suggested for mathematics, creative writing, physical education, art, model-making and drama. These are practical ideas which can be used and developed on individual lines by teachers. They are given as instances of how assessment may be undertaken, and are not to be regarded as accepted measuring instruments.

4 Children's Creative Ideas and Their Evaluation

The most popular way of evaluating creativity in children during the last decade has been by means of CREATIVITY TESTS. The first tests were developed by Guilford and his associates at the University of South California. The theoretical background to these tests, and an account of their historical development was given in Chapter 1, pp. 22–25. They were closely linked with Guilford's work on the structure of intellect, and were particularly aimed at identifying and evaluating divergent thinking abilities as suggested in his structure of intellect model. Torrance and other workers at the Bureau of Educational Research, University of Minnesota, developed Guilford's early work on testing and applied many of his ideas to the needs and interests of children. The work at Minnesota assumed that creative thinking was not an entity in itself, but rather made up of complex patterns of abilities, such as Guilford's primary traits of creativity, i.e. sensitivity to problems, fluency of ideas, flexibility of thinking, originality, elaboration, and redefinition. Thus measurement is usually in terms of marks for fluency, flexibility, originality, etc. The reason for this is that creative people are generally considered to be sensitive to their surroundings, both human and physical, and so they recognise problems and begin thinking about them. They have many ideas (fluency) and can communicate them. They can envisage a width or variety of ideas on a single topic (flexibility), and are able to produce ideas which are different from those produced by others (originality).

Creativity tests are as yet very unsophisticated measures of creative ability. If a test is said to have a high coefficient of reliability, it means that when it is given to the same group of children on different occasions the results are similar. This cannot be said about creativity tests. Generally speaking, they do not have high coefficients of reliability, although steps have been taken to improve test reliability which have had some success. Similarly, if a test is said to have good validity, it means that there is strong evidence that it does actually measure what it is supposed to do. Again, there is only very limited evidence that creativity tests do actually measure creative abilities. This whole problem was discussed in some detail in Chapter 1, p. 24. However, it is true that over the last few years tests of creativity have become progressively more reliable and valid. The findings of early workers have been adapted, and their ideas have been refined and built on by other investigators. It is essential that teachers know that creativity tests are now in the stage of evolution; that they are still subject to modification and adjustment. There are many ways of scoring creativity tests. No one method is to be considered correct or conclusive. It is possible for teachers to devise their own scoring schedules to produce the information they require. Generally speaking, it will be found preferable to follow an established, clearly defined scoring pattern, and adapt this to individual needs if this is necessary. To a generation of teachers brought up on the very rigidly defined marking schemes of tests of verbal reasoning and achievement, where no deviation was allowed, the ideas outlined for marking creativity tests will seem most unorthodox. It must be remembered, though, that it is the very inflexibility of marking in normal objective tests, which precludes the marker from rewarding a deviant answer which may be highly original and creative.

The development of marking and scoring rationales is crucial to the further refinement of creativity tests, but it is unlikely that one system will emerge which will effectively preclude the use of all others. Much remains to be learned about scoring these tests, and it is possible that useful information will come from the empirical findings of teachers working in the classroom as well as researchers working under the strict experimental conditions of a specific research design.

Creativity tests are very varied in form. Some are based on a verbal stimulus and response, others on a non-verbal stimulus and verbal response, and yet others are non-verbal tasks with non-verbal stimuli. In devising marking schemes for these tests, researchers are concerned to reflect all the abilities used by the children in constructing their answers. Scoring procedures, however, do have to be simple enough to operate easily. As it is rarely possible to be definite about all the answers which are to be rewarded, there is a subjective element in most marking systems. However, as I illustrated in Chapter 2, even for rating creative activities high estimates of inter-rater compatibility can be obtained. In creativity tests investigators have often reported inter-marker compatibility coefficients above $+0.85$.

In order to give teachers the complete information needed to administer and mark some creativity tests, three verbal tests will be given in detail, together with a scoring scheme; and three non-verbal tests will be similarly treated. Other tests devised by various investigators will then be briefly indicated and a reference given so that these may be followed up if desired. All the tests given here have been used and adapted by successive researchers whose contribution is acknowledged.

VERBAL TESTS OF CREATIVITY

The three tests described here derive from the work of Guilford. They are presented using a format developed by Wallach and Kogan (106) which has been slightly adapted for use in English schools. The scoring scheme given is also based on the work of Wallach and Kogan.

1 *Instances*

Instructions for administration

Say: 'In this game I am going to tell you something and it will be your job to write down as many things as you can think of that are like what I tell you. For example, I might say 'things that hurt'. Tell me some things you can think of that hurt. [Take answers on a 'hands-up' basis.] Yes, those are fine. Some other kinds of things might be falling down, slapping, fire, bruises or a knife. [Delete or add to as necessary.]

'So we see there are all kinds of different answers in this game. Do you see what you have to do? . . . Good. I think you are all set to begin. *Remember* – I will name something and you are supposed to name as many things as you can think of that are like what I have said. You will have plenty of time. I will wait until people seem to have finished before going on. Don't worry about spelling; just do the best you can. The spelling is not important. It is your ideas I am interested in. Let us begin.

1 Name all the round things you can think of.
2 Name all the things you can think of which make a noise.
3 Name all the square things you can think of.
4 Name all the things you can think of which move on wheels.'

NB. – It will be found helpful if children number their lists, or if their answer paper has been divided or folded in such a way that identification of each group of answers is easily made.

Instances task: marking instructions. The test can be marked for fluency and originality (uniqueness).

Fluency. This is defined as the total number of responses given by a child to a particular item, e.g. name all the round things you can think of: clock, cups, ball, bottle bottom, orange, grape, pennies.

Seven responses: fluency score, 7.

The score for the procedure as a whole is the total responses for the various items in the procedure.

Originality (Uniqueness). This is defined as follows: For each item in a procedure a frequency distribution is constructed to indicate the number of children in the group who give a particular response to that item. This analysis is carried out for every response provided to that item. Any response to a given item that is offered by only one out of the total sample is defined as unique (original) response. The number of unique (original) responses provided by a child in his answers to a particular item constitutes his uniqueness score for that item. A child's uniqueness score for the procedure as a whole consists of the sum of his uniqueness scores for the various items which constitute the procedure.

N.B. – The criteria for originality can be altered so that a child who gives a response which is given by a certain percentage of the group might be rewarded. This percentage may be 10 per cent or even 20 per cent, depending on the use to be made of the results. Obviously, if a child has to make a response which no other child makes and the number in the group is large the possibility of giving a unique response is limited. A general rule may be: the larger the group the better the case for making the criterion for assessment less exacting.

Torrance has used weighted scoring systems, as have many other investigators, but any system like this involves a rigorous try-out and careful analysis of the results before weightings are decided upon. In fact, Wallach and Kogan (106) concluded that 'Initial analysis indicated that orderings of children based on the present definition of uniqueness [i.e. the one given above] are highly similar to those that result from the more arduous approach of assigning weights to all responses in terms of relative infrequency of occurrence'.

2 *Alternate uses*

Instruction for administration

Say: 'In this game I am going to name an object – any kind of object, like the light bulb or the floor – and it will be your job to write down lots of different ways this object could be used.

'Any object can be used in a lot of different ways. For example, think about *string*. What are some of the ways you can think of that you might use string? [Take answers on a 'hands-up' basis.] Yes, those are fine. I was thinking that you could also use string to attach to a fishing-hook, to skip, to sew with, to hang clothes on and to pull a truck along. [Delete or add to as necessary.] There are lots more too, and yours were good examples. I can see you already know how to play this game. You will have plenty of time. Write your answers simply: e.g. to skip, to sew with, to hang clothes on. And don't worry about spelling. Concentrate on as many different ways you could use the object I name as you can. Let us begin.

1 Tell me all the different ways you could use a *newspaper*.
2 Tell me all the different ways you could use a *knife*.
3 Tell me all the different ways you could use a *cork*.
4 Tell me all the different ways you could use a *shoe*.
5 Tell me all the different ways you could use a *button*.
6 Tell me all the different ways you could use a *key*.
7 Tell me all the different ways you could use a *chair*.
8 Tell me all the different ways you could use a *tin can*.'

N.B. – Marking will be made easier if the children are given answer papers which have been numbered to correspond with the eight items in the procedure.

Alternate uses: marking instructions. The test can be scored in a very similar manner to that outlined for the 'Instances' procedure, namely for *fluency* and *originality*.

As in the former test, the scorer will assess the number of unique responses in the manner already detailed for each item. These results will be summed to obtain an *originality* score for the instrument as a whole.

The *fluency* score is the total number of responses that a child gives to each item. These are summed to yield the number of responses for the procedure as a whole.

3 *Similarities*

Instructions for administration

Say: 'In this game I am going to name two objects, and I will want you to write down all the ways that the two objects are alike. I might name any two objects, like *door* and *chair*. But whatever I say, it will be your job to think of all the ways that the two objects are alike. For example, tell me all the ways that an apple and an orange are alike. [Take answers on a 'hands-up' basis.] That's very good. You've already said a lot of things I was thinking of. You could also have said they are both round, they are both sweet, they both have seeds, they are both fruits, they both have skins, they both grow on trees – things like that. [Delete or add to as appropriate.] Do you see how we play the game? Yes. I think you do.

'Write your answers simply, e.g. both have seeds, both have

fruits, and don't worry about spelling. Concentrate on finding many ways that the two objects are alike. Let us begin.

1   Tell me all the ways in which a potato and a carrot are alike.
2   Tell me all the ways in which a cat and a mouse are alike.
3   Tell me all the ways in which a train and a tractor are alike.
4   Tell me all the ways in which milk and meat are alike.
5   Tell me all the ways in which a supermarket and a cafe are alike.
6   Tell me all the ways in which a violin and a piano are alike.
7   Tell me all the ways in which a radio and a telephone are alike.
8   Tell me all the ways in which a watch and a typewriter are alike.
9   Tell me all the ways in which a curtain and a rug are alike.
10 Tell me all the ways in which a desk and a table are alike.'

N.B. – Again, numbered or divided answer sheets facilitate marking.

Similarities: marking instructions. This test can also be scored for fluency and originality. The procedure will follow the manner already described. Scores on each item can be added to give total scores for fluency and originality for the task as a whole.

NON-VERBAL TESTS OF CREATIVITY

Introduction

The three tests described in this section are all from 'The Minnesota Tests of Creative Thinking' developed by the Bureau of Educational Research, University of Minnesota. Several forms of all these tests are available. See Torrance (93). The scoring scheme given is that suggested by Yamamoto (113). In his work Yamamoto stresses the experimental nature of his scoring procedures and shows the need for further development of them. They are included here in a form which is simple and systematic. Teachers will find that, with a little practice, marking will become both quick and efficient. Markers should become familiar with the categories by making a few trial markings before any organised scoring is attempted. This will pay dividends ultimately.

1 *Figure completion*

Instructions: 'By adding lines to the two figures below, draw some object or design. Try to think of some object or design that no one else in the class will think of. Try to include as many different ideas as you can in your drawing. In other words, don't stop with your first idea for completing the figure; keep building on to it. Make up a really good title for each of your drawings and write it at the bottom of each block next to the number of the figure.'

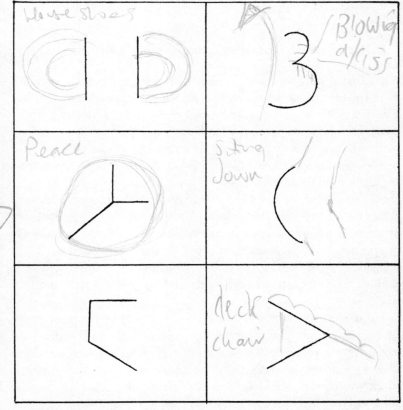

N.B. – This test is sometimes used as a timed test taking ten minutes. In practice it can be used untimed. Children usually finish in about ten minutes.

Incomplete figures task: marking instructions

This test will be scored to achieve a grade for fluency, flexibility, originality and title adequacy.

Fluency

A score for fluency is obtained simply by counting the number of responses a subject completed and/or gave a title. (In effect, most children attempt all six and this score is seldom of any real value in an untimed test. Occasionally it does indicate real rigidity.)

Flexibility

Each response is to be classified into one of three categories:

1   *Life–nature (denoted by L).* Any response representing organic life or inorganic nature in any form. This category thus includes plants and their parts, animals and their parts, birds and their parts, fish and their parts, human beings and their parts, as well as natural elements, such as sky, sea, cloud, star, mountains, etc.

2   *Ornamental–household (denoted by O).* Any response representing daily household or decorative items which, however, exclude those belonging to the third category. The distinction between these two categories depends on uses of an item, presence or absence of a more or less self-contained energy source, possibility of spontaneous movement and other similar considerations. This second category thus includes furniture, decorative articles, tableware, clothes, processed foods, drugs, sports goods and the like.

3   *Scientific–mechanical (denoted by S).* Any response representing mechanical constructs or scientific instruments and appliances which imply more or less self-contained energy sources and/or spontaneous movements. This category thus includes various kinds of vehicles, ships, air-going vessels, bridges, roads, buildings, electrical and mechanical instruments and appliances and the like. Parts of these articles, such as coil, condenser, bolt, cog, beam and picture tube of T.V., are also included here.

Flexibility is obtained quite simply by counting the number of runs in terms of these three symbols. By definition, responses are so ordered as to follow our normal reading habit, top left to top right, middle left to middle right, etc., e.g.

O	O	4 O's – 1 run
O	O	2 S's – 1 run
S	S	

Flexibility – 2

L	O	1 L – 1 run
O	S	2 O's – 1 run
S	L	2 S's – 1 run
		1 L – 1 run

Flexibility – 4.

Originality. This is the sum of the weighted scores given each response according to the basic principles (perception patterns) revealed. The table below presents the two principles and the weights given them under each category of flexibility. These weights are based upon the responses from 211 pupils in kindergarten through Grade 6 of an elementary school in Minnesota.

'Symmetry' represents such a pattern of response as to result in a symmetrical completion of the stimulus figure. Any figure which has any axis of symmetry should be classified under this principle.

'Asymmetry' represents all those responses in which picture completion was carried out in such a way as not to result in symmetrical figures.

Principles to be used in scoring for originality (figure-completion) and weights to be given

Categories for flexibility	Principles for originality	Scoring weight
Life–nature (L)	Symmetry Asymmetry	1 4
Ornamental–household (O)	Symmetry Asymmetry	1 4
Scientific–mechanical (S)	Symmetry Asymmetry	2 4

Title adequacy. The scorer is to pay attention to titles given, not pictures drawn, and to evaluate their expressiveness.

Score	Description	Example
0	No title given	
1	Simple label or name of drawn objects without any modifier	Snowman, rocket, balloon
2	Label or name of drawn objects with descriptive modifiers	Frosty the Snowman Upside-down house
3	Imaginative title which expresses feelings, reactions and descriptions over and beyond what can be seen in the picture	What beautiful wallpaper! Who gets the next spanking?

2 *Picture construction*

Instructions: 'You have been given a piece of paper in the form of a triangle. Think of a picture you can draw with this form as a part. Your drawing can be anything you like and you can do it anyway you like. The shape is gummed. Stick it wherever you want it on this sheet of paper and add lines with pencil or crayon

....

Title: ....

to make your picture. Try to think of something no one else in the class will think of. Keep adding things on to it, putting into your picture as many interesting ideas as you can. When you have completed your picture, think up a name or title for it and write it at the bottom. There is no time limit, but we think it will take you about ten minutes.'

Picture construction task: marking instructions
Three scores, originality, elaboration and title adequacy, are derived from responses.

Originality
A score for originality is determined by the principle with which the subject utilised the coloured sheet in making up his picture. The table below presents the fundamental principles (categories) to classify a response into and weighted scores to be given.

Explanation of terminology
'*Simple figure*' represents those uses of the coloured sheet in which no addition to speak of was made to the sheet in constructing a picture. Quite often the sheet is simply pasted on to the answer sheet without any elaboration whatsoever and a title given, e.g.

SIMPLE FIGURE

Life–nature: cloud, pond, lake, sun, potato
Ornamental–household: hot-dog, hat, rug, cake
Scientific–mechanical: boat, canoe, sleigh, bomb

'*Structural part*' covers those responses in which the sheet was used in such a fashion as it make it part of a larger structure. Often, simple additions are made to the sheet to make, for example:

STRUCTURAL PART

Life–nature: human or animal body, tree, human mouth
Ornamental–household: umbrella, flower-pot, candle-holder, skirt
Scientific–mechanical: bus, aeroplane, submarine, train, wagon

'*Field*' covers those responses in which the coloured sheet was used as field for a figure inside of it. Examples include:

FIELD

Life–nature: human or animal face, garden
Ornamental–household: cage, flag, target, design
Scientific–mechanical: tunnel, thermometer, traffic-lights

Principles to be used in scoring for originality (picture construction) and weights to be given

Category	Principles involved	Scoring weight
Life–Nature (N)	Simple figure	10
	Structural part	5
	Field	10
Ornamental– Household (O)	Simple figure	10
	Structural part	10
	Field	15
Scientific– Mechanical (S)	Simple figure	5
	Structural part	10
	Field	15

Elaboration

A response is considered for its elaborations and given a score according to the following scheme:

Score	Description	Example
0	No elaboration beyond the minimum essentials to represent and convey what a subject has in mind	Car: two wheels added Lake: nothing added
5	Elaboration of picture elements *outside* of the coloured sheet	Space-ship, house
10	Elaboration of picture elements *inside* of the coloured sheet	Tent: windows added inside Flag: design added inside
15	Elaboration of picture elements both *inside* and *outside* the coloured shape	Man: head, etc., outside; clothes, etc., inside; buttons etc.

Title adequacy

In scoring for this dimension, the scorer should pay attention primarily to titles given and judge them for their expressiveness.

Score	Description	Example
0	No title given	
1	Simple label or name of the drawn object *without* any modifier	Hat, canoe, flower, lake
2	Label or name of the drawn objects *with* descriptive modifier	An Indian out for a ride. My mum's new hat. Top view of a table
3	Imaginative title which expresses feelings, reactions and descriptions over and beyond what is seen in the picture	I will cook for you. The bread that fell in the red dye. Out for a ride. Beat that if you can

3 *Circles*

Instructions: 'In ten minutes see how many objects you can make from the circles below. A circle should be the main part of whatever you make. With pencil or crayon, add lines to the circles to complete your picture. Your lines can be inside the circle, outside the circle, or both inside and outside the circle. Try to think of things no one else in the class will think of. Make as many things as you can and put as many ideas as you can in each one. Add names or titles if it is hard to tell what the object is.'

Marking instructions

Circles. Three scores, fluency, flexibility and originality, will be derived from this test.

Fluency

A score for fluency is obtained simply by counting the number of responses given, excluding only those responses repeated in identical form. Because of the difficulty in some instances of deciding whether a response (circle) is completed or not, count

every response regardless of the degree of perfection (completeness) of the response.

Flexibility

Flexibility score, as defined here, is the number of runs revealed in responses in terms of the following three categories:

1 *Life–nature* (L). Any response representing organic life or inorganic nature in any form. Thus this category includes such responses as plants (flowers, trees, grasses, fruits, etc.), animals

and their parts (faces, legs, etc.), birds and their parts, fish and their parts, human beings and their parts, in addition to such responses as cloud, sky, rain, snow, sea, lake and the like.

2 *Ornamental–household* (O). Any responses representing daily household, or decorative items which, however, do not imply any more or less self-containing energy sources and/or possible movement. This category thus includes such responses as ball, coin, container, clothes, frying-pan, decoration, design, drugs, processed foods and the like.

3 *Scientific–mechanical* (S). Any response representing mechanical constructs or scientific instruments, tools and other items which imply more or less self-containing energy sources. This category thus includes such responses as bridge, building, ship, car, rocket, man-made satellite, as well as such ones as clock, TV, radio, radar, barometer (dial instruments), movie-projector, telephone, refrigerator and the like. Parts of these articles are also included here (e.g. washer, condenser, hub-cap, etc.).

Each response is to be classified into one of those categories, L, O or S, and then flexibility is obtained quite easily by counting the number of runs in terms of these three symbols as detailed for flexibility in the Incomplete Figures Task.

Originality

Originality, as defined here, is the sum of the weighted scores given each response according to the basic principles (perception

*Principles to be used in scoring for originality (circles)
and weights to be given*

Categories for flexibility	Principles for originality	Scoring weight
Life–nature (L)	Figure	2
	Field	3
	Structural parts	4
Ornamental–household (O)	Figure	1
	Field	3
	Structural parts	4
Scientific–mechanical (S)	Figure	4
	Field	3
	Structural parts	4

patterns) revealed. The table above presents these principles classified under each of the three categories used in deriving flexibility, and weights to be given to each of these.

In the above table 'Figure' represents a category (pattern of perception) in which a circle is seen and used as a simple figure in a larger but unspecified ground. Some examples are listed below.

FIGURE

Life–nature: sun, moon, Saturn, earth, apple, flower
Ornamental–household: letter 'O', ball, coin, pie, record
Scientific–mechanical: hub-cap, bell, bulb, lens, globe

'Field', on the other hand, represents a category in which a circle is seen and used as a field in which to describe other 'figures'. For example,

FIELD

Life–nature: human or animal face, eye, half-moon
Ornamental–household: fish-bowl, target, umbrella-top
Scientific–mechanical: bicycle, glasses, house

'Structural parts' represents a third category in which the circle is seen and used as part of a larger structure. For example:

STRUCTURAL PARTS

Life–nature: human body, animal body
Ornamental–household: snowman, pipe, dumb-bell, bracelet
Scientific–mechanical: bicycle, glasses, house, TV set, traffic lights

Brief descriptions of some other creativity tests

VERBAL TASKS

Torrance (93) describes the following tests:

1   *Impossibilities*

The instructions simply state: 'List as many impossibilities as you can think of.' The answers were scored for fluency (the number of relevant responses), flexibility (the number of different categories of impossibilities) and originality (any responses other than a list given by Torrance as not being original).

This test was originally used with adults by Guilford and adapted for children by Torrance, who expresses some doubt about using the scoring practice given here.

2 Consequences

This is another task developed from Guilford's work. In Form A children were asked:

(a) What would happen if a man could become invisible at will?

(b) What would happen if a hole could be bored through the earth?

(c) What would happen if the language of birds and animals could be understood by man?

In Form B the questions were:

(a) What would happen if the days were twice as long as they are?

(b) What would happen if a man could live forever on the earth?

(c) What would happen if men could fly without mechanical aids?

Torrance used this as a timed test (five minutes for the three problems combined). He scored this for fluency, flexibility and originality, using the same pattern as the Impossibilities task.

3 Just suppose

The children are shown a drawing of an improbable situation accompanied by a verbal description. They then have to think of all the other things that could happen because of it. For example, two improbable situations used are:

(a) Just suppose our shadows were to become real.

(b) Just suppose the picture you drew became real.

Scoring follows much the same pattern as for the other tests described.

4   *Situations*

Children have to think of as many solutions as they can to such problems as 'If all schools were abolished, what would you do to try to become educated?'

5   *Common problems*

Children are asked to think of as many problems as they can which might arise in connection with everyday situations, such as taking a bath or making a sandwich.

6   *Improvements*

Common objects, such as bicycles, shoes and coats, are given. Children have to suggest ways of improving them.

7   *Mother Hubbard problem*

Children have to think of all the things Mother Hubbard would have done when she found there were no bones in the cupboard.

8   *Cow-jumping problem*

Similar to the Mother Hubbard problem, in this task children have to think of all the things which might have happened when the cow jumped over the moon.

Hudson (49) used a test which he called 'Meaning of Words'. The same test was used by Getzels and Jackson (32) and was called 'Word Association' by them. Children have to write down as many meanings as they can for a list of words which includes bit, bolt, duck, fair, fast, pink, pitch, port, sack and tender. Hudson also describes a test called 'Controversial Statements' which he used with grammar-school pupils. Children are given some controversial statements, such as 'The happiest years of your life are spent at school', or 'Science fact will soon be stranger than science fiction'. They pick out those which interest them and comment on them as they think fit.

Yamamoto (113) describes other tests developed at Minnesota.

The first is called 'Ask', and involves showing children a picture. They have to ask questions about the picture, and are encouraged to ask imaginative and creative questions (e.g. 'Those questions you would need to know to understand what is happening, not questions which can be answered by just looking at the picture'). 'Guess Causes' is a test where children have to guess anything which might have caused the action in the picture, while in the test called 'Guess Consequences' the idea is to suggest possibilities of what might happen as a result of what is happening in the picture.

These brief descriptions show the type of problem posed for this kind of test. This list is by no means exhaustive. Teachers could easily make up unusual ideas which pose a thinking situation for the children and which might elicit a creative response. In fact, once they are used to the idea, some children are exceptionally apt at devising these tasks. So, besides providing a vehicle for testing creative abilities, these situations may provide novel ideas which the creative teacher and class may develop imaginatively to produce a wealth of original responses over a wide area of the curriculum.

NON-VERBAL TASKS

There have been many attempts to assess creativeness over the years, but these efforts have been mostly in the artistic sphere. Hence many of these tests were non-verbal and involved drawings, ink-blot interpretation and transformation of objects by elaborating them. Torrance (93) identifies many of these efforts in some detail.

It should be pointed out that the three non-verbal tests described in detail have alternate forms. Other figures have been used as alternatives to those given earlier. The idea of using incomplete figures, outside the test context, in order to present children with a stimulus for creative thinking may well commend itself to some teachers. Any figures used should be capable of extension, have a quality of ambiguity, and be open to a wide range of possible interpretation.

In the picture-construction task, a curved shape has been used instead of a triangle in some investigations.

The circles test described can be presented with a series of squares instead of circles. I have found that with younger children more difficulty is posed by the squares than the circles, and results are generally less fluent.

Various attempts have been made to devise tasks of creative design. These have usually had the common basis of giving a series of gummed shapes which have to be assembled into a picture or design. Scissors have been provided by some investigators to allow children to cut the shapes for more individual and original use.

Hudson (49) and Getzels and Jackson (32) both used simple drawing tests. They asked children to draw a picture to illustrate a given title, e.g. 'Zebra crossing', 'Playing tag in the school yard'. Scoring is difficult and involves a large element of judgement. However, a suggested method of doing this for paintings has already been described in Chapter 3.

Wallach and Kogan (106) used two non-verbal tests based on the work of Tagiuri (87). Pattern meanings is a task where children are shown drawings capable of varied interpretation.

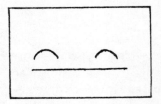 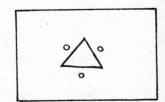

The examples given show the type of illustration used. Marks are given for fluency (the number of patterns interpreted), and originality (how unique they were). Teachers will be aware that the production and interpretation of figures of this kind is a popular pastime amongst children.

INTERPRETATION OF THE RESULTS OF CREATIVITY TESTS

Teachers regularly use ideas similar to those used in creativity tests in their everyday classroom work as stimuli for creative problem-solving and to evoke imaginative responses. This is natural, and provides some indication that intuitively teachers are providing the same opportunities for the exercise of creative abilities that researchers are using to systematically assess them. However, teachers may see the need to use creativity tests more directly sometimes. How should the results be interpreted? It should be borne in mind that any test samples only a minute part of the creative thinking abilities of a child, and caution is needed in making any interpretation. The profile obtained from the results of a wide range of tests is probably more reflective of the child's creative capabilities than any one measure. Thus tests may be used to indicate ability over a wide field of creative activities, and be used to try to make some tentative identification of creative talent in a variety of pursuits. It seems likely from research that children who are given a wide range of tests will present an uneven profile of results in scoring highly in some and low in others. It will be rare for a child to have consistently high marks and ratings over a series of tests if the aspects they cover are diverse.

Possible follow-up to the administration of creativity tests

A very detailed review of how the teacher can encourage creative talent has been given by Torrance (93,96), and it is not the intention here to replicate any of this work. My aim is to look specifically at certain courses of action which may follow from examining the results of a series of creativity tests. If a child shows real potential in an area of creative activity, this needs to be encouraged very systematically. More work can be provided, and a careful attempt should be made by the teacher to present challenging material which will help to raise the level of creative thinking involved and also introduce the pupil to new skills which will be the tools of his further creative expression. It is my view that where ability is seen it should be rewarded and re-inforced, and a degree of excellence established. A case can be made out for giving extra help where test results have been poor, but if this is done motivation is likely to be limited and interest-level will probably be low. I prefer to take the course of action suggested and have found that the success experienced and the high level of ability reached eventually have the effect of raising abilities in other spheres. What has happened is that better self-concepts and self-awareness have been established and the other tasks have been approached more positively.

Where pupils are successful in a creative activity, it seems likely that they think easily in the area. They have what can be described as an affinity with the media. To put it another way, they see the problem in heightened relief, and are able to suggest many original answers to it. It is possible that the problem is suited to what has been called 'the INDIVIDUAL COGNITIVE STYLE' of the person. The role of the teacher is to try to identify the pupil's 'individual cognitive style'. No pat, easy way of doing this can even be suggested. However, many teachers would testify that if they analyse carefully a teaching situation where they have been particularly successful, this is probably what has happened. They have, at the teaching moment, been 'tuned in' to the individual's own way of thinking and have been able to help the pupil to see old relationships in new lights. It is from situations like this that further creative thinking can emerge and be developed.

SUMMARY

A short summary of the development of creativity tests is given and ways in which these can be used by teachers are suggested. In order that teachers can administer some of these tests, full administration details and marking procedures are given for a series of verbal and non-verbal tests. Short descriptions of a range of other tests are given and references to obtain more details of these are included. Some help is given in how to interpret results of creativity tests, action which may be taken and pitfalls to avoid. Caution is urged, but experimentation is encouraged. Ideas to follow-up after tests have been administered are included.

5 An Analysis of Some Creativity Test Responses

In this chapter pupils' creative responses collected from tests of creativity will be reviewed. This will enable teachers to compare the responses given by their own children with those presented and discussed here. Any comparisons made will be subjective, but they may be very useful in helping to appreciate how creative ideas are engendered and expressed. It may also be useful to study answers given in tests of creativity to see whether they represent creative responses when assessed against one's own intuitive ideas of what constitutes 'a creative response', as distinct from adhering strictly to a marking schedule.

VERBAL TESTS OF CREATIVITY

Instances

In this test pupils were asked the following questions:

1 Name all the round things you can think of.
2 Name all the things you can think of which make a noise.
3 Name all the square things you can think of.
4 Name all the things you can think of which move on wheels.

Common responses to Question 1 (round objects) were as follows:

apple	buttons
ball	cake
balloon	circle
bottle	cylinders
bucket	chips
bulbs	eye(s)

eyeballs	pan
face of clock or watch	pencil
glasses	plant-pot
globe	plate
gobstopper	plugs
hole	records
inkwell	ring
jar	saucer
letter O	sun
marbles	tyre
milk-bottle top	watch
moon	wheel
orange	

Responses which were given by only one pupil in the sample were as follows:

drain-pipe	postmark
fish-bowl	orb
cabbage	Stonehenge
melon	the effect of a moving fan
ice-rink	waist
dome	boiler
dandelion-head	

In this test pupils who specified particular articles tended to score well according to the marking system used. For example, 'sweet' was common, whereas 'rum truffle' was uncommon. In one respect, these responses 'beat' the marking system more than they represented real originality. Unusual fruits scored for originality, while common fruits did not.

There was a connection between verbal fluency and originality on this test which showed through the effective use of words. In this context, the word 'brim' was used to describe a cup (brim of a cup). This was unique (the common response was just 'cup') because of the facility in using an unusual description of the top of the cup.

Evidence was available when results were individually studied that fluency of response was associated with originality. Pupils with many responses certainly seemed to produce more original ones. This does support Guilford's findings on this point.

Common responses to Question 2 (things which make a noise) were as follows:

aeroplane	guitar	sea
babies	guns	ship
bees	hammer	shouting
bells	laughing	singing
bird	lion	siren
bus	motor-bike	talking
car	me	tape-recorder
cat	mouth	telephone
chairs (on floor)	musical instruments	television
children	people	thunder
clock	piano	tigers
coughing	pigs	train
cow	radio	trumpet
crying	rain	violin
dog	recorder	water
door	record-player	whistle(ing)
drum	rockets	wind
elephant feet	screaming	wireless

Unusual responses were as follows:

human beings	falling plate
matches	rattlesnake
chisel being used	bursting ball
fire	computers working
echoes	

Common responses to Question 3 (square things) were as follows:

blackboard	book
box	brick
calendar	ceiling
cage	chair
clock	cube
cupboard	desk
dice	door
fish-tank	floor
house	map

mat	paper picture
rubber	radio
sink	square inch
square yard	square foot
table	television
tile	tin
walls	window

Unusual responses were as follows:

an acre	car sliding roof
ceiling trap-door	sliced bread
oxo	decorative candles

Responses in this section were less fluent and more inhibited. The concept of 'square' seemed less productive than the other stimuli given. This is also reported by investigators using squares as distinct from circles in the circles non-verbal test. The test did produce a crop of humorous responses, one being a reference to a teacher's head, which showed a degree of perceptive accuracy and imaginative application, if it didn't strictly merit a mark!

Common responses to Question 4 (things which move on wheels) were as follows:

ambulance	pram
baby-walker	roller-skates
bed	scooter
bicycle	settee
blackboard	stage-coach
bus	table
car	tank
caravan	toys
chair	tractor
coach	trailer
crane	train
go-cart	tricycle
lawnmower	trolley
lorry	van
motor bike	waggon
piano	wheelbarrow
plane	wheelchair

Unusual responses were as follows:

cement-mixer   turntable
combined harvester   hospital bed
pit cages   sand yachts

The number of unique responses to this item was very limited, and pupils seemed to find it difficult to think outside accepted frames of reference.

Alternate uses

In this test pupils were asked the following: 'Tell me all the different ways you could use a newspaper, knife, cork, shoe, button, key, chair, tin can.' Below are set out the common responses for each item. Unusual responses are discussed afterwards.

1 PAPER

to back books	for identification tabs
make book-marks	to get information
for burning	to make a kite
to make a bird-cage	as a door-mat
covering up things	for masks
for doing crosswords	to measure
to make dresses	to paint on
to make decorations	to make cases
for doll's-house furniture	for papier mâché
to make fire	to screw-up
to float	for stuffing
to make hats	to keep warm
to throw away	sell it
to use as trumpet	for wiping things
to use as umbrella	as a weapon
to waft	to put into worn shoes

2 KNIFE

to cut	to operate
for carving	as a pin
as decoration	as pincers
envelope-opener	to prise open
harpooning	to peel
as a hammer	as a spade
to model material	instead of screw-driver

to shave
to sell
to trim a beard
as an aerial
to pop balloons

for Scouting
to throw
as tin-opener
use as weapon
to pick locks

3   CORK

as a buoy
in bars
to blot ink
as a button
use as ear-plug
instead of door-stop
float for fishing
to repair shoes
as a lifebelt
to model
use in necklaces
for puppetry
for rubbing-out
for filing roof

on a cricket bat
to make balls
to chew
to make a compass
as a protector
in experiments
eyes for snowmen
to gag someone
as a missile
for mouse-traps
use as pin-cushion
plant-pot
as a swimming aid
target

4   SHOE

for the dog to play with
as a boat
as a charm
to block open a door
as fuel
for making footprints
to play games
to use as hammer
imaginative play
as a souvenir
as a swatter
as skates
to throw
as a vessel
for warmth
to bail out

as bait
a cup
for decoration
for dancing
to hold flowers
for fish-tanks
to hide things in
for living in
to take off another shoe
as a purse
to squash things
as a target
use as tool
instead of a teapot
to wear as a hat
as a weapon

5 BUTTON

to burn	to count with
to buy in make belief	to draw around
as switch on a pen	decoration
for a bell-push	to eat
as a charm	as doll's eyes
to play games	flying saucers
as a missile	to make necklaces
to make mosaics	for pellets
to play shove-halfpenny	to make patterns
to race them	to sew on
to roll them	to spin
to play yo-yo	to toss

6 KEY

to switch on an alarm	to hide
to clean nails	to jangle
for copying	to lock
to indent clay	to lose
for decoration	as a light (map-key)
to hang round neck	to open things
as a pendulum	to point
to use as die-stamp	to throw
as 21st present	to wind-up
to use as weight	to stop a nose-bleed

7 CHAIR

to break	to carve
to burn	as a coat-hanger
as a boat	to defend yourself
to balance on	as a den
for electrocution	as a door
to light fire	for French-skipping
to hide something under	for karate practice
to use in taming lions	as ladders
for musical chairs	to clean windows on
to mend	to paint
as a shield	to sit on
to help teach swimming	to stand on
to lean against	for sleeping
to tie people to	as a table

8 TIN CAN

as a bomb
to balance on
as a cup
as a measure
as a cylinder
to make holes in
to hide something
as knife
as loud-hailer
to make miniature garden in
to play with
as petrol tank
to smash
as scrap
as stilts
to stamp on
to saw
as a mallet
as a target
to use as chair-leg

for a dustbin
as a drum
to carry fish
to play games
to make a groove
as a hat
to kick
as receptacle
to help in modelling
to open
to paint
as a pan
to put radio in
to roll
to race
to make a shape
to throw it
to tie on a cat's tail
to make telephone
to make shapes with

The responses for alternate uses were very much more predictable, and there was less originality. Paper used for testing out pens, to wrap up a bomb and to use as a cork were unique responses. A knife used to burst a tyre and to strip wallpaper were also unique. Using a cork to make a thermometer and to make a person sick were original responses. Shoes attracted no original responses, while using a button as ammunition was unique. Melting down keys for the metal was an original answer, as was using a chair to test the quality of a spring. There were no wholly original uses for a tin can.

Buttons appeared to present most difficulty for pupils in this sample. Responses were few and stereotyped, whereas a key was very successful.

It was noticeable that some pupils applied their ideas to all the objects: it was possible to apply an idea to nearly all the articles. For example, 'to use as a weapon' applied to most, as did 'use as a receptacle'. In fact, many original responses were sparked off in this way by applying ideas to many articles.

Eight articles were used here. On reflection, it seems that this may be too many for optimum response. The fluency and originality of the responses was less as the pupils became tired and possibly bored.

As has been noted in other contexts, where there was fluency of response there was also more originality.

Similarities

In this test pupils were asked to state all the ways in which two articles were alike. The common responses for representative sections are given below:

1 POTATO AND CARROT

vegetables	have green shoots
eaten with salads	can be sliced
have roots	solid
grow below ground	can be stewed
can be eaten raw	grow in England
can be canned	have eyes
neither is sweet	oblong-shaped
cheap	need washing before eating

2 CAT AND MOUSE

have noses	sharp claws
pointed ears	have babies
four legs	breathe air
like to keep warm	mammals
can be pets	fight
wild or tame	chase prey
move quietly	have good scent
playful	friendly
wary	eyes shine at night

3 TRAIN AND TRACTOR

have engines	can go fast
made of steel, etc.	let off steam
have wheels, etc.	bump up and down
carry people	pull things
give off fumes	have 't' in name
man-made	are vehicles
are transport	are driven

I

move	heavy
are painted	need fuel
observe speed limits	make noise
can be used as toys	used for public service
often seen	start with switches
take us somewhere	go past fields
obey laws	are washed
not alive	not mammals

4 MILK AND MEAT

good to eat	feed us
can be cooked	come from cow
can be refrigerated	have protein
start with 'm'	have vitamins
part of human diet	from animals
bought from shop	have skin
are dairy produce	smell
have colour	are eaten in school
nourishing	have four letters
can be boiled	digestible
soft	go stale

This test was more difficult for less able children, many of whom were unable to write any answers at all. It requires the ability to generalise and abstract to a high degree of sophistication, and would require the child to think in operational terms.

Some children misunderstood the brief and wrote generally about the two articles. Two children concentrated on differences and produced such responses as, 'The mouse is small, but the cat is big.' It may be assumed that these children did not interpret the instructions correctly. Certainly they could not be rewarded by marks under the marking system used. Their work did show some ingenuity, though. This is a problem with devising any task to measure creativity. The same task context which is used to assess creativity may also inhibit it. Along with the criterion problem, this represents a serious weakness of creative assessment, and illustrates that both objective tests and personal opinion may have to be used ultimately in the total assessment of creative abilities.

NON-VERBAL TESTS OF CREATIVITY

Incomplete figures

This test is described on p. 101, and involves adding lines to six incomplete figures.

Three marks were extracted from the drawings: flexibility, originality and title-adequacy. I shall examine pupil's work to show high-scoring responses for each of the marks.

The highest possible score for flexibility is 6. Elaine's drawings (shown in Figure 1) are very immature artistically. When they are categorised, however, they show complete flexibility in terms of the scoring schedule (see pp. 102–4). The responses are as follows:

1	Scientific–mechanical	1 S
2	Life–nature	1 L
3	Scientific–mechanical	1 S / 1 L
4	Life–nature	1 L
5	Ornamental–household	1 O
6	Scientific–mechanical	

Six 'runs' in all.

The highest possible score for originality is 24. In the scoring schedule (given on p. 103), responses are weighted for symmetry and asymmetry. Most children complete the figures symmetrically. In Phillip's drawings, shown in Figure 2, he has avoided what could have been symmetrical figures by elaborating on his original drawing in pictures 3 and 4, and by the hand and fish in picture 6. This elaboration, although not marked separately, has given him a high originality score, and was suggested in the instructions, '. . . keep building on to it'.

Figure 1

Name: Elaine. *Class:* 5. *School:* . . . *Ref.:* JF/MCED.

Instructions: By adding lines to the six figures below, draw some object or design. Try to think of some object or design that no one else in the class will think of. Try to include as many different ideas as you can in your drawing. In other words, don't stop with your first idea for completing the figure; keep building on to it. Make up a really good title for each of your drawings and write it at the bottom of each block next to the number of the figure.

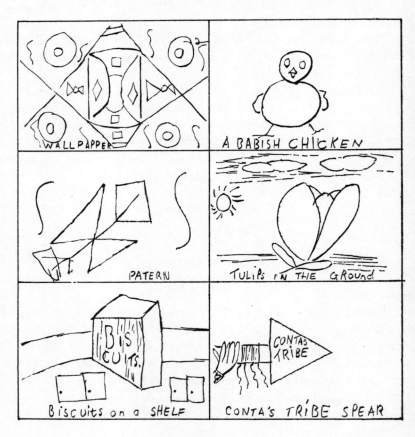

Figure 2

Name: Phillip. *Class:* 1. *School:* . . . *Ref.:* JF/MCED.

Instructions: By adding lines to the six figures below, draw some object or design. Try to think of some object or design that no one else in the class will think of. Try to include as many different ideas as you can in your drawing. In other words, don't stop with your first idea for completing the figure; keep building on to it. Make up a really good title for each of your drawings and write it at the bottom of each block next to the number of the figure.

The highest possible score for title adequacy is 18. This would require six imaginative titles which express feelings, reactions and descriptions over and beyond what can be seen in the pictures. No pupil in my sample gained full marks. Many expressive titles fufilling these conditions were given. Examples of these are given below:

> The lonely snowman thinking of summer
> The uncounted biscuits

Where does the ancient train go ?
Man overboard!
Unbelievable
Find the centre of the city
Jump, if you can
Not too many
Just a little
Fire out, etc.

Picture construction

This test is described on pp. 104–7, and involved making a picture using a coloured shape as a part.

Three marks were extracted from the drawings: originality, elaboration and title-adequacy. Pupils' responses will be examined to show high-scoring responses.

It is significant that no pupil in my sample scored the maximum marks for originality. This would have involved producing a picture with either an ornamental–household, or scientific–mechanical theme where the principle of construction was 'field', i.e. the coloured sheet was used as field for a figure inside it. Examples of this would be:

household: cage, flag, target
scientific: tunnel, thermometer, traffic lights

The fact that no pupil produced this type of response does support Yamamoto's view that it is rare. However, this does not seem surprising to me, since the instructions ('keep adding things on to it, putting into your picture as many interesting ideas as you can') would lead normal, lively children of this age to elaborate outside the shape given. However, it is conceded that the ability to resist doing this is rare, and may pick out originality. Once more the criterion becomes hotly debatable.

Many children produced responses which attracted 10 marks, the next highest group. An example of one of these is shown in Figure 3, which illustrates the marking for elaboration as well.

Figure 3

Name: Gordon. *Class:* 7. *School:* . . . *Ref.:* JF/MCED.

Instructions: You have been given a piece of paper in the form of a curved shape. Think of a picture you can draw with this form as a part. Your drawing can be anything you like and you can do it anyway you like. The shape is gummed. Stick it wherever you want it on this sheet of paper and add lines with pencil or crayon to make your picture. Try to think of something no one else in the class will think of. Keep adding things on to it, putting into your picture as many interesting ideas as you can. When you have completed your picture, think up a name or title for it and write it at the bottom. There is no time-limit, but we think it will take you about ten minutes.

ITS AN EVERY DAY LIFE

The highest possible score for elaboration is 15. A great many children scored top marks in this section. This involved elaboration of the picture elements both inside and outside the coloured shape. It would be impossible, under this scoring system, to gain maximum marks for elaboration and originality. It may be argued that this is also a disadvantage of this marking system.

Many responses showed a dominant interest in space and moon monsters. Gordon's picture (Figure 3) is scientific–mechanical, has good elaboration and contains an expressive title.

The highest possible score for title adequacy is 3, the criterion being the same as for the Incomplete Figures test. Examples of good, imaginative titles were as follows:

> A footballer celebrating his team's goal
> Join us on the swing
> 'Oh! What a lovely raincoat, Mandy'
> The German's defence falls
> Home from the wars
> An awning in Paris looking on to the Eiffel Tower
> 'Operation Moon!' Moon Station – 2167
> Invasion on Pluto from Mercury
> The famous jockey rides again
> Hair of different animals and parts of their body

Circles

This test is described on p. 107, and involves drawing objects from circles.

Three marks are extracted: fluency, flexibility, and originality. Pupils' responses will again be examined to show high-scoring responses.

Fluency scores (counting the number of responses made) were high. Most pupils attempted nearly all the circles in the same way as Steven in the example given in Figure 4.

The highest possible score for flexibility is 30. It would be very unusual for a child to have 30 'runs'. Steven's drawings, shown in Figure 4, merited a flexibility score of 21. This is typical of high-scoring responses for flexibility. He has been able to change his frames of reference easily, and his responses, classified L, O, and S, show this well.

The highest possible score for originality is 120. Steven's score of 76 was in the top 5 per cent of results from my sample. It shows an ability to think outside the very common ideas for responses, such as balls, coins, pies, records, the sun, the moon, apples, flowers and planets. Ability to use the circle as part of a larger structure, which Steven does well on several occasions, is unusual and is rewarded as originality.

In this test it was interesting to note that younger children, aged 9 years, generally used the circle as field in which to draw other 'figures'. Their responses were mostly like Anthony's (Figure 5), who only drew anything outside the circle on very rare occasions. Nevertheless, many of his responses are unusual and his originality score is high.

Figure 4

Name: Steven. *Class:* 2. *School:* . . . *Ref.:* JF/MCED.

Instructions: In ten minutes see how many objects you can make from the circles below. A circle should be the main part of whatever you make. With pencil or crayon, add lines to the circles to complete your picture. Your lines can be inside the circle, outside the circle, or both inside and outside the circle. Try to think of things no one else in the class will think of. Make as many things as you can and put as many ideas as you can in each one. Add names or titles if it is hard to tell what the object is.

Figure 5

Name: Anthony. *Class:* 2. *School:* . . . *Ref.:* JF/MCED.

Instructions: In ten minutes see how many objects you can make from the circles below. A circle should be the main part of whatever you make. With pencil or crayon, add lines to the circles to complete your picture. Your lines can be inside the circle, outside the circle, or both inside and outside the circle. Try to think of things no one else in the class will think of. Make as many things as you can and put as many ideas as you can in each one. Add names or titles if it is hard to tell what the object is.

Figure 4

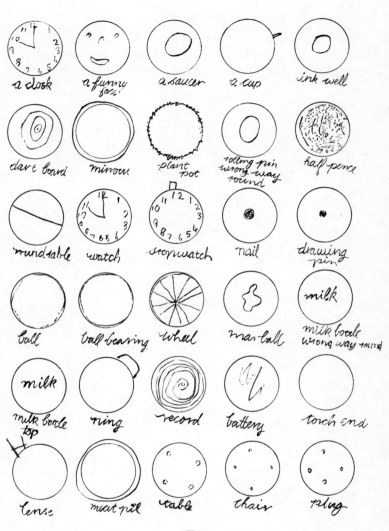

a clock   a funny face   a saucer   a cup   ink well

dart board   mirror   plant pot   rolling pin wrong way round   half pence

round table   watch   stopwatch   nail   drawing pin

ball   ball bearing   wheel   marble   milk bottle wrong way round

milk bottle top   ring   record   battery   torch end

lense   meat pie   table   chair   plug

Figure 5

Figure 6

Name: Karen. *Class:* 5. *School:* ... *Ref.:* JF/MCED.

Instructions: In ten minutes see how many objects you can make from the circles below. A circle should be the main part of whatever you make. With pencil or crayon, add lines to the circles to

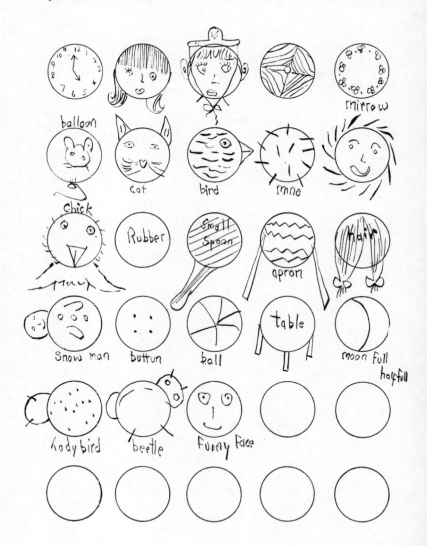

complete your picture. Your lines can be inside the circle, outside the circle, or both inside and outside the circle. Try to think of things no one else in the class will think of. Make as many things as you can and put as many ideas as you can in each one. Add names or titles if it is hard to tell what the object is.

This test did produce many completely individual responses. Jonathan, aged 9, saw all the circles as road-signs and completed them as such. Shelley, aged 9, saw them all as faces and drew thirty different faces. This naturally depresses the flexibility score completely, but high scores in fluency and originality could still be obtained. Martin's drawings were all mathematical. Many were decorated with the geometric parts of a circle, some were counters, coins, and others were the background on which he drew mathematical signs.

The responses of girls were quite different from the boys. Karen's work (Figure 6) can be compared with the boy's work shown earlier. The femininity of her response shows clearly in the rather cute, pretty faces, the hair, and the accent on household objects, like a spoon and a mirror.

SUMMARY

Pupils' creative responses in both verbal and non-verbal tests of creativity are presented and examined. The advantages and short-comings of the marking systems used are discussed, and an indication is given of whether tests are likely to prove fruitful as assessing instruments for pupils during the middle years of schooling.

Teachers may find the responses which are given useful for comparing with those obtained from their own classes. The responses may also provide a guide to some of the ways in which creative thinking may be encouraged by showing common and unusual frames of reference used by some children. By studying these teachers may be able to help the children to think outside normal lines, and become more adventurous in producing ideas.

6 Identification of Creative Ability by Self-ratings, Teacher-ratings and Peer-ratings

In Chapter 1 (p. 29) I gave a description of some of the attempts which have been made to identify creative abilities by self-ratings, teacher-ratings, and peer-ratings. From this summary it is clear that investigators have found real difficulty in devising measures which would indicate creative ability, using the ratings of teachers and pupils. However, I believe that teachers can be helped to gain a fuller knowledge of their pupils by developing questionnaires which show how the pupils regard their peers, what they think about their own abilities, and how they react to their work. Basically, therefore, this chapter will outline my own attempts to formulate a means of identifying creative ability by using ratings. The limitations of this approach are clearly acknowledged, and where objective data regarding the reliability and validity of the instruments is available it is included. I suggest that the measures have little to recommend them purely as instruments which may pick out creative ability in pupils, but I do think that they are valuable in assisting teachers to obtain data which can help them to re-think the principles which govern their work, enable them to plan more fruitful stimuli to invoke creative response and assist them in seeing their pupils through the eyes of their peers.

SELF-RATING OF CREATIVITY

I constructed the following questionnaire using criteria established by Torrance (93) on the characteristics of the creative personality. Questions, suitable for 9–11-year-olds, are based on attributes said by Torrance to differentiate highly creative persons from less creative ones. For example, one characteristic is said to be that the creative person rejects repression. This is represented by the sentence on the blackboard.

There are no right or wrong answers. Just answer as you did then by deciding if the sentence fits you.

This is a secret quiz and no one in your school will see the answers. The quiz is to try to find out what children think about themselves and the things they do.

						Creative characteristic	Negative or positive	Indices of discrimination
1	I think I am tidy	Yes	No	Don't know	1	Accepts disorder	N	0·22
2	I like to know what other classes in school are doing	Yes	No	Don't know	2	Aware of others	P	0·44
3	I like to explore new places with my parents better than on my own	Yes	No	Don't know	3	Adventurous	N	0·38
4	I like to be best at something	Yes	No	Don't know	4	Desires to excel	P	0·44
5	If I have some sweets, I usually keep them all	Yes	No	Don't know	5	Altruistic	N	0·33
6	I get mad with myself if the work I do is not my best	Yes	No	Don't know	6	Discontented	P	0·22
7	I want to find out how everything works	Yes	No	Don't know	7	Full of curiosity	P	0·38
8	I am not popular with other children	Yes	No	Don't know	8	Not popular	P	0·5
9	I sometimes act 'babyish'	Yes	No	Don't know	9	Regresses	P	0·33
10	If I want to do something, being smacked would'nt stop me	Yes	No	Don't know	10	Rejects repression	P	0·44
11	I prefer working with others and never like working by myself	Yes	No	Don't know	11	Likes solitude	N	0·27
12	I know when I can do something really well	Yes	No	Don't know	12	Self-confident	P	0·27
13	Even though I think I am right, I change my mind if everyone else thinks I am wrong	Yes	No	Don't know	13	Independence	N	0·44
14	I worry a lot if I make mistakes	Yes	No	Don't know	14	Makes mistakes	N	0·38
15	I am often bored	Yes	No	Don't know	15	Never bored	N	0·22
16	I shall be important and well-known when I grow up	Yes	No	Don't know	16	Sense of destiny	P	0·33
17	I like to look at beautiful things	Yes	No	Don't know	17	Sense of beauty	P	0·33
18	I prefer games I know rather than making up new games	Yes	No	Don't know	18	Self-starter	N	0·5
19	I like to find out: What will happen if I do something?	Yes	No	Don't know	19	Speculative	P	0·44
20	When I am playing out I take very few risks	Yes	No	Don't know	20	Willing to take risks	N	0·40
21	I like watching TV better than doing this	Yes	No	Don't know	21	Thrives on activity	N	0·27

statement, 'If I want to do something, being smacked wouldn't stop me.' Similarly, 'a sense of destiny' is reflected in the comment, 'I shall be important and well-known when I grow up.' Included with the questionnaire are the list of creative characteristics associated with each statement, an indication of the positive or negative use of the statement, and the INDICES OF DISCRIMINATION which were obtained in constructing the questionnaire. Instructions for administration and marking details are given fully so that teachers can use the questionnaire if they wish to do so.

QUESTIONNAIRE: SELF-RATING OF CREATIVITY

Instructions for administration

Write on the blackboard:

I like puzzles	Yes	No	Don't know
I like my own way most of the time .	Yes	No	Don't know

Read the instructions on the children's form, pointing out that if the sentence fits them, i.e. they like puzzles, they underline 'Yes'; if it doesn't fit them, they underline 'No'.

They use 'Don't know' if it is applicable, but the teacher should stress that for most sentences they will probably be able to decide easily if it fits them or not.

Repeat this with the second sentence on the blackboard and then begin the questionnaire. (It is probably easier for the teacher to read each question in turn and allow the children to select their answer, thus eliminating the poor-reader problem.)

Marking instructions

Eleven questions are positive, requiring a 'Yes' response for a mark; 10 questions are negative, requiring a 'No' response for a mark. The placing of positive and negative questions was by random selection. Positive questions are indicated by P, negative by N.

One mark for a 'Yes' response to a positive question, 1 mark for a 'No' response to a negative question. A marking template can easily be made by cutting out the correct response so that if a pupil has indicated this answer, it is immediately apparent.

The reliability of the questionnaire

The following technical details are included so that interested readers can assess the questionnaire in psychological terms:

The following estimates of reliability were obtained:

1   Split half (corrected) $r = 0.69$ ($N = 54$)

This coefficient was obtained by correlating scores on the odd numbered items with those on the even numbered items.

2   Kuder Richardson $r = 0.71$ ($N = 54$)

The questionnaire was originally used in try-out with 38 items. An item-analysis was carried out when scripts were arranged in order of total score and divided into equal thirds. Indices of discrimination were then established for each item. Using this index, 17 items having indices of less than 0.22 were excluded and 21 items were retained.

The same data allowed an estimate of reliability to be made using the Kuder-Richardson formula. Using all the original items, the internal consistency coefficient was $r = 0.42$ ($N = 54$).

When only the 21 items having the highest indices of discrimination were used, as given here, this was raised to $r = 0.71$ ($N = 54$), as quoted above.

The test re-test reliability of this questionnaire was established as follows:

$$r_{11} = 0.46 \ (N = 49).$$

PEER-RATING OF CREATIVITY

The questionnaire used to try to obtain a peer-rating of creativity is again based on the work of Torrance (93) and his so-called

K

dimensions of creativity. It is sociometric in form, and asks for nominations of children who best fit certain statements. For example, children are asked, 'Who, in your class, has the most wild and silly ideas?' Three spaces are given for the answer and children can therefore give up to three nominations. As I indicated in Chapter 1, I decided to widen the scope of earlier work in this field and ask children to answer questions to try to find out who they thought were popular, conforming, and had leadership qualities, as well as trying to obtain an assessment of creative qualities.

In course of try-out, using 54 pupils, the following estimate of test re-test reliability was obtained:

$$^r 11 = 0.98 \ (N = 54)$$

QUESTIONNAIRE: PEER NOMINATION OF CREATIVITY AND OTHER ATTRIBUTES

Instructions for administration

The questionnaire is self-explanatory. It is found helpful if the names of the children in the class are written on the blackboard so as to aid spelling. The teacher may wish to read through all the questions first in order to help if any in the class are slow readers:

Here are some questions about your class. Write down three names in answer to each question if you can. One or two names will do if you cannot think of three. Don't worry about the spelling of the names. Just write the names as well as you can. Most of the names are on the blackboard if you wish to copy them.

This is a secret quiz. The other children will not see your answers. It is to help to find out about children's interests, ideas and games.

1 Write down the names of your three best friends.
2 Who in your class talk most about their own ideas?
3 Who in your class can think of the most interesting, unusual things to do when you have time to play?
4 When you are playing, if something happens to spoil your game or stop your enjoyment, who in your class would be

the first to think of a way of solving the problem so that you could start playing again?

5 Who in your class is best at making up new games to play?
6 Who in your class has the most wild and silly ideas?
7 Which children in your class never get into any kind of trouble?
8 Which children are the best team leaders for school work?
9 Which children are the best team leaders for games?
10 Did you enjoy answering these questions? Put a ring round your answer. Yes. No. Don't know.

Marking instructions

From this questionnaire it is possible to acquire a rating in each of the undermentioned qualities numbered 1 to 5.

1	*Popularity*	Give 1 mark for each nomination in Question 1. Record the total nominations for each child.
2	*Creativity*	Give 1 mark for each mention by name in Questions 2, 3, 4, 5 and 6. Add these and record the total nominations for each child.
3	*Conformity*	Give 1 mark for each nomination in Question 7. Record the total nomination for each child.
4	*Leadership* (*school work*)	Give 1 mark for each nomination in Question 8. Record the total nominations for each child.
5	*Leadership* (*games*)	Give 1 mark for each nomination in Question 9. Record the total nominations for each child.

N.B. – How many children enjoyed answering the questionnaire and how many disliked it? Were there any 'Don't knows'?

TEACHER-RATING OF CREATIVITY

In my study I asked each class teacher to rate children in the sample in the following factors or areas of creative thinking: fluency, originality, flexibility, inventiveness, elaboration.

The criteria to be used were set out simply for each variable in non-technical terms, e.g.:

Fluency. To what extent does the child show the ability to produce an abundance of ideas, the emphasis being on *quantity*?

I drew up these criteria initially using the descriptions of the divergent thinking factors noted by Guilford (38, 39) which were said to identify areas of creative thinking. The same dimensions are used extensively by Torrance (93) in the development of sociometric criteria. In this case the dimension was used, but the criteria were adapted to teacher-rating.

The following guide to assessment of creativity was given to teachers:

The teacher is asked to rate each child in the sample in the following factors or areas of creative thinking: fluency, originality, flexibility, inventiveness, elaboration.

Guide to assessment
The children should be listed in rank order on each factor.

Fluency
To what degree does the child show the ability to produce an abundance of ideas, the emphasis being on *quantity*?

Originality
To what extent does the child show the ability to produce unusual and clever responses showing originality and an element of uniqueness in both formal and informal situations, within and outside school?

Flexibility
To what degree does the child show the ability to deal with the environment in a flexible way? Is the child good at solving a problem in a variety of ways? Does he/she resort to the uncon-

ventional easily? Are problems looked at in a wide context, thus allowing for flexibility in solving them?

Inventiveness

To what extent does the child show the ability to generate ideas which present a new, challenging and thought-provoking aspect: ideas which have quality, are constructive and produce in the onlooker feelings of astonishment and surprise?

Elaboration

To what extent does the child show the ability to build on a simple idea? Is she/he able to see the difficulties and consequences involved in a problem which is being developed? To what extent is the child, when given a lead, able to elaborate on it?

THE USE OF SELF, PEER AND TEACHER-RATINGS OF CREATIVITY

The limited reliability and validity of this form of rating has already been indicated. However, the use of these questionnaires can be fruitful. Research has often indicated that teachers' assessments of creative ability are biased towards children's verbal/educational abilities. They are generally more accurate in predicting achievement than creativity. Perhaps, though, we should not expect teachers' ratings to show a close relationship with creativity tests. After all, the test samples only a very narrow field of creative response whereas, no matter how stringent the criteria, the teacher will bring global judgements to bear in making any specific assessment. Overall, the teacher takes a wider view, based on a variety of uncontrolled variables embodied in past experience, in making judgements of creative potential. The bias of teacher estimates towards attainment and attitudes in school could be explained in terms of Mackworth's (62) view which distinguishes between problem-solvers and problem-finders. Teachers are far more often involved in assessing children in the former rather than the latter situation and so, in Mackworth's terms, are perhaps better equipped, through experience, to identify the convergent rather than the divergent thinker. A teacher who is aware of these tendencies may be in a better position to make more unbiased, objective assessments.

The data gathered from the self-rating questionnaire of creativity may give some indication of children's interests, self-concepts, preferences and likely behaviour in certain circumstances. This information can be used by an astute teacher, particularly in an informal learning environment, to arrange for work which is more fully appropriate to the individual pupil. For example, answers to statements like 'I am often bored', 'I worry a lot if I make mistakes' and 'I prefer working with others and never by myself' may provide an insight into behaviour which the teacher may not have noticed before.

In my study there was some evidence (through the existence of peer-nomination variables on certain creativity factors) that pupils may be better at recognising creative abilities in manipulative, non-verbal fields than teachers. They seemed to associate ability in manipulative fields with creative ability and ability in academic subjects with conformity. In an active classroom the give-and-take of peer-group conversation, which brings out ideas which are different from those which would be engendered by the teacher, should be encouraged. Many examples have been given where the stimulus for creative thinking has come from a prompt by the teacher. Here I want to highlight the stimulus which can arise from the pupil's own discussions. Their insights into each other's modes of thinking and abilities can generate fruitful ideas which often lead tangentially to imaginative work.

A group of 12-year-old boys were working on a surveying exercise in the park. They had gathered data but were having considerable difficulty in working out a suitable scale to present their findings in map form. After several abortive attempts, Simon suggested they should ask Alan, who was working with another group, to help, because 'he's good at maths and also at doing small drawings in his book from posters'. This bizarre combination of abilities hardly looked to me to be likely to produce an answer to their problem. I did not know this group well, but I had been watching and helping them with their work in the park that afternoon. However, I had declined to give further help beyond that which had enabled them to reach the point at which

Alan was brought in. I was surprised when Alan arrived, firstly by the efficient way he was briefed about the problem by Simon and, secondly, by the suggestions he made in quick succession. He gave two boys a measurement to calculate how they would represent it on a 1:10 scale and see whether it would fit their paper. Another boy worked on 1:20, and another on 'call chains inches'. After a discussion of this, they decided to make two maps, each involving a different scale, so that they could show a particular small area in more detail than the rest. All this work grew from a knowledge of a boy's particular abilities by one of his friends. I believe that it is probably this incidental use of peer opinion which will ultimately benefit the teacher most. However, discussion must be allowed to develop in an atmosphere where pupil's own opinions are valued and dialogue is encouraged. I have been working in a similar context today with mature students in a college of education, and I noted exactly the same principles at work in their problem-solving as I have described in the group of 12-year-old boys. Similarly, in discussion with a colleague, it was pointed out to me that a scoutmaster will usually notice different abilities in a group of boys than a teacher could pick out with the same group. It may be that all participants in a group accumulate different sets of information about the group members, all of which can be used positively to help the group in the right circumstances.

SUMMARY

An attempt to identify creative abilities using self-ratings, peer-ratings and teacher-ratings is described. The questionnaires used are given in detail so that they can be used by teachers. It is suggested that the data gathered from the self-rating questionnaire may give some indication of children's interests, self-concepts, preferences and likely behaviour in certain circumstances. Peer-nominations of creativity gained from the questionnaire may be useful to the teacher in providing a completely different view of the capabilities of a group of children from that held by the teacher. The limitations of teacher-ratings of creativity are outlined, but possible reasons for this are discussed. The fact that a teacher is aware of these limitations may put him in a better position to make more unbiased, objective assessments.

The limited reliability and validity of this approach is acknowledged.

7 Creativity, the Pupil and the Teacher

In Chapter 1 the characteristics of the creative personality, as seen by a wide range of researchers, were outlined. However, the point was made that no inclusive description was likely to fit any individual in total. It is more likely that teachers will meet children who show only some of the traits, said to be associated very strongly with the creative personality. Creative behaviour in school will often cut across accepted standards of conduct. If a child is an original thinker and full of imaginative ideas, it follows that some of his behaviour will appear to be somewhat deviant and certainly unconforming. This can create a clash between the pupil and the teacher. The outcome of this may be resentment, forced conformity, rebellion or 'an opting-out of the system'. Direct confrontation of this kind must be avoided. If teachers are aware of some of the outward signs of a creative personality, and concerned to nurture this, freedom to express creative desires will be given. This is in no way a suggestion that there must be no control or systematic guidance: in fact, the directive is quite the reverse. Effective guidance is necessary through the provision of appropriate materials, and control is necessary so that pupils with creative potential experience the boundaries within which they can both adventure and also feel secure. It is important that these boundaries are wide, that they are flexible and that they are not inhibiting, but nevertheless they will be there. They will, however, not be enforced by an authoritarian relationship of teacher to pupil, but rather supported by a relationship based on consideration for the individual.

CREATIVE BEHAVIOUR IN THE CLASSROOM

In order to illustrate the role of the teacher in eliciting creative response, to show some of the complexities of pupil/teacher interactions and to highlight the need for both sympathy of approach and effective action by the teacher, several classroom encounters will be analysed and discussed. These illustrations are reported as they were recorded at the time. Teachers and students who were involved in this work operated on a team basis so that detailed recording could be undertaken.

Suggested aspects of the creative personality, as detailed in Chapter 1, had been noted. In discussion we had wondered whether these traits could be identified in children in classrooms, and whether, in fact, they could be shown to be associated with creative endeavour.

WORK ARISING FROM A DISCUSSION OF COMIC STRIPS

The teacher had been discussing comic-strip techniques of story-telling. She produced some prepared strips where the climax was left to their imagination. Various possible endings were then discussed in the group. Other stimuli were introduced for discussion subsequently; usually in the form of such questions as: 'What would happen if a cat had puppies?', 'What would you do if the force of gravity failed for one hour?', 'What would you do if every time you touched wood you couldn't let go?'

The children in this group were 10–11 years and ranged in ability from average to high.

Following the initial presentation of material and long discussion, some children wrote stories, others recorded their ideas on tape, while others just talked about possible endings and courses of action amongst themselves. This work was analysed by the teacher, who read the stories herself on to a tape. This was played back while the children listened. One story was called 'Susan, spring onions, and the uncivilised man, Harlequin'. This original title was given to a story concerning Susan, who ate some spring onions delivered to her in a parcel. They had a magical effect on her. The following comments occurred after this story had been read. They followed the question, 'What else do you think the onions might do?'

Martin: 'They could talk.' (Bisociation.)

Russell: 'Have babies.' (Bisociation and adventurous thinking.)

Russell: 'The babies could have babies. There could be an Old Onion's Home.' (Openness to the irrational.)

Martin: 'They could have eyes.'

Adele: 'Go to different parts of the country.'

Beverley: 'Could have tails.'

Martin: 'They could have ears.'

Adele: 'We are making up the story. They could do anything we wanted them to do.'

(Willingness to toy with ideas.)

The comments below followed the open-ended situation at the end of Katharine's story about the ballet shoes that could dance by themselves. 'How could they do it?'

Alan: 'Springs on the bottom.'

Martin: 'Clockwork.'

Russell: 'A diddy computer in the heels.'

Russell: 'They could have feet themselves.'

(Resourcefulness.)

Martin: 'They haven't got eyes. That's how they got knocked over.' (Martin showed great fluency – many ideas.)

Russell: 'Six feet each make up for losing eyes.'

Alan: 'With six feet they could run faster.'

Nigel: 'You wouldn't know where to run.'

Martin: 'You could feel.' He then showed us how this could be done.

Question interposed here: 'Where would the eyes be?'

Beverley: 'In the laces at the end.' (Originality.)

Question interposed: 'What colour might they be?' Several colours suggested but –

Alan: 'They would be a special colour.' (Attraction to the unknown.)

Russell: 'There could be a built-in radar like bats.' (Exploratory thinking.)

Martin: 'Like your head beating.' (Element of ambiguity at this
   point.)

Then, later,

Martin: 'Radar is just like your head in a way.' (Exploratory
   thinking.)
Martin: 'Something must make the radar beat.' (Attraction to
   the unknown.)

These notes reveal a wealth of creative thinking. They also
show how many of the traits said to be associated with creative
thinking are present in children when they have problems to solve.
However, the interaction of the teacher with the well-timed,
carefully-posed question does guide the thinking and is a great
spur to further original thought. The need for the teacher to be
able to identify possibilities for creative development and know
how to encourage this is clearly illustrated here. It will be noticed
that many of the responses could cause laughter, disruption and
general unruliness in children of this age. It is a mark of the
success of these teachers that they were able to handle a potentially
negative response, and ensure that not only was it accepted
positively by the group, but in itself sometimes became a spur for
further creative ideas. The following examples from the same
group again illustrate aspects of creative functioning which were
identified in the written work which came from the same stimulus:

ASPECTS OF CREATIVE THINKING REVEALED IN
CHILDREN'S WRITTEN WORK

Martin: 'The Red Genie and the Pirates.'

   Martin personified himself as 'the genie of the red eye'.
   His description of the eye was '. . . a red eye, soft as jelly.
   . . . It was not a human eye – it was a magic eye.' (Fluency,
   originality and elaboration.)

   'I wish the pirates would turn to stone . . . and their boat
   would turn to water.' (An interest in primary processes.)

   On completion of his story, Martin asked if he could paint
   a picture of the eye, and, immediately after completing

this, asked if he could make a model. He sorted through the collâge materials saying aloud, 'I need something red and spongy.' (Ability to toy with materials and also exploratory thinking.)

Beverley: 'The Dogs that Purred.'

'. . . and only one dog was left, a lonely one. The other dogs laughed, you could see from their faces.' (Sensitivity.)

Gillian: 'Susan, Spring Onions, and the Uncivilised Man, Harlequin.' (Originality.)

After eating spring onions delivered in a parcel, Susan '. . . begins to walk up the walls and swing from the lamp-shade.' (Wild and silly ideas.)

'Susan put a notice in the newspaper. It said: "Spring onions found. Owner please collect. No reward need be given." ' (Resourcefulness.)

Katharine: 'Barbara and the Mysterious Shoes.'

Katharine was the only child to leave her story open-ended, posing the question '. . . One thing Barbara still had to solve . . . how the shoes could dance by themselves.' (The ability to be puzzled, and to live with an unsolved problem.)

Beverley: 'The Coat Stand that got Married.' (Originality.)

The coat-stand in the story runs away, dressed in a coat and hat, and passes a church, where it sees a bride and groom. It then goes to a scrapyard, where it meets another coat-stand (in dress and veil and holding a bouquet of flowers!) The two then go to the church and ask the Vicar to marry them. (Bisociation.)

WORK ARISING FROM PAINTING

The group had been listening to a tape as a stimulus to painting (in much the same way as outlined in Chapter 3).

The following notes are particularly concerned with the personality characteristics said to be associated with creative people. The teachers were keen to try to find examples of these traits, and analyse whether they were useful in the creative activity being undertaken.

Ability to regress

'The boys showed little fluency, flexibility or originality during the initial painting. However, when they were given large sheets of textured wallpaper and asked to paint they gained confidence. They made swirls and shapes with the brush over and over until a mud-pattern emerged. They enjoyed doing this and it did seem that they needed this regression before they could return to the more disciplined approach of their earlier activities.'

Receptivity

'There was a different reaction to the playing of the tape from the boys to the girls. The former were restless at first, giggled and played around. The girls were serious and concentrated. On the second playing, the boys changed, listening intently, and made notes to help them later with their painting. We thought they all achieved an element of receptivity (which seemed to be required for this activity) eventually.'

Sensitivity

'Fiona showed sensitivity in choosing materials for the collâge. For the monster she asked me, "Have we got something that looks scaly?" She chose a silk material that was exactly right to create this effect.'

'Fiona remarked whilst stroking a piece of fur on the collâge, "If we hang this up, everyone will want to stroke this fur."'

'The way the model *felt* was very important particularly to Michael. He wanted a smooth dome to the head, and attempted to smooth the plaster with sandpaper. This failed. But then he discovered a new way to use the paste and achieve the effect he required. He considered the placing of the eyes at some length, as the expression they gave was important. He said, "I want him to look soft, you know, sad and gentle."'

Tender-mindedness

'Fiona, explaining to me about the two monsters she and Jane had created: "This horrible one is going to catch this nice little one with a big net. Everyone likes this little one." '

The ability to toy with materials

'Both Fiona and Jane gave a lot of thought to choosing materials. Jane wanted to create some rock in one corner. "For things to crawl on," she said, and she tried out several ideas, e.g. black screwed-up tissue paper, orange cellophane, cellophane tissue, etc., until she found the effect she wanted.'

WORK ARISING FROM DRAMA

The group of children had drawn a map which was the key to treasure. They wanted to act out the finding of this treasure. They had many ideas, had produced the map themselves, and worked out ideas which could be developed dramatically. However, they were unable to co-ordinate their efforts in order to dramatise the ideas. Adult intervention was necessary here. The teacher organised groups, properties, and spaces for each activity in the hall. A discussion of exactly how to set about acting-out the story followed. Afterwards the work developed quickly and ingeniously. I saw the children at work, and was impressed by their concentration, co-operation and skill in mime. It was incredible that the arguing, quarrelling group I had seen earlier could have been so transformed. In fact, it had taken skilful guidance, and careful planning, by the teacher before this highly creative group activity could take place at all: it was as if a key had been turned which had unlocked all the potential. Further support is lent to this by the fact that many times teachers involved in this work reported that, left completely to their own devices, with no suitable leads, pupils tended to lose interest and made little progress. A system which gives complete, step-by-step guidance inhibits the pupils' ability to proceed imaginatively themselves; likewise, complete freedom seems equally unfruitful in engendering adventurous responses. With children of this age the teacher, using the principles of guided discovery learning, does seem to facilitate the ability to produce optimum creative response.

The teachers involved recorded many examples of creative thinking similar to those already given. Their list included illustrations of bisociation, the ability to seek out and combine knowledge in new ways, innovation, exploratory and original thinking, sensitivity, apprehensiveness and the ability to break away from some of the crippling restraints of conformity.

ENCOURAGING CREATIVITY IN THE CLASSROOM: THE COLLATED VIEWS OF A GROUP OF TEACHERS

The following points are a summary of the opinions of a group of teachers who held a seminar on the topic, 'How can the teacher encourage creative responses in the classroom?' They reflect the thinking of teachers from primary and secondary schools, many of whom held widely differing views on their role and the aims of education. They are included here principally as discussion points and as a basis for individual reflection. They are not in any order of priority.

1   A good pupil/teacher relationship is essential. Views differed on the precise nature of this relationship, but it was agreed that the teacher must be a good listener, receptive to ideas and be able to respond positively to them.

2   Co-operation should characterise group activities, and competition should not be used as the main spur to effort.

3   Time-limits should rarely be used, but teachers should be aware of 'pace' in pupils' learning. Effective use of a knowledge of the pace at which individuals work should promote creative response. It is acknowledged that indiscriminate use of pace as a spur to effort would have the reverse effect.

4   It is essential that the teacher arranges for pupils to be successful. The implications of this for the building up of positive self-concepts were considered important..

5   There should be a significant emphasis on participation by the pupils in planning their own work.

6   The rewards which should be aimed for should be concerned ultimately with the intrinsic satisfaction of having done something

really well. If this approach is adopted, external incentives will cease to be necessary.

7 'Efficient organisation' in the classroom will be concerned with basic order and routine. The organisation of pupils' learning will be extremely flexible, allowing individual choice, discrimination and judgement.

8 Most learning will be undertaken on an integrated basis, bringing in related disciplines as they arise naturally.

9 There should be little objective testing and direct evaluation involving the pupil. Progress will be assessed by the teacher independently. Where discussion takes place with a pupil about his work, the teacher will emphasise positive elements, and 'encouragement' will characterise the teacher's approach.

10 There will be an emphasis on the provision of a wide variety of material in plentiful quantities. This is more important than sophisticated technical equipment during the middle years of schooling.

11 Pupils' own ideas will form the basis and starting-point of their work. Discussion about these should be encouraged. Brainstorming techniques* could be used to produce ideas.

12 Many starting-points for study will be outside school, which should be regarded as a 'base for learning' rather than the 'seat of learning'.

13 There should be time for pupils to browse.

14 The teacher should have in mind the needs of a balanced programme without making this known to the class.

15 Problems should be given which are solved in groups. Collaboration is important and often gives rise to new ideas which can be developed by individuals.

16 A team-teaching approach is likely to be fruitful. The team could profitably include students, aides and auxiliaries.

17 It is important to build up learning resources. Creative work makes great demands on background material.

18 Begin from where the pupils are, not where the teacher thinks they ought to be.

19 Let the pupils go to where they want rather than where the teacher thinks they ought to go.

* For full details see Freeman, Christie and Butcher (28).

20   The use of educational games which call for imaginative, individual solutions has great potential for creative development which has not really been used fully yet.

Examples of

SUMMARY

Creative ability may show itself in school in many ways. Illustrations of children's creative behaviour are given, analysed and discussed. It is suggested that the teacher is a crucial factor in nurturing creative response. Much potential is only realised if the teacher is able to recognise creative behaviour, and is subsequently sympathetic towards it and makes active efforts to cater for it and encourage it. This will probably best be accomplished in an atmosphere where the individual is respected and genuine participation is encouraged, the teacher joining in and carefully guiding the pupil's thinking so that further original ideas are the outcome.

L

8 The Ability Explosion

Much of this book has been concerned indirectly with the nature
and structure of human abilities. Until comparatively recently
most teachers in England have regarded ability in terms of
academic achievement and verbal reasoning. From much of the
research concerned with creativity, it appears that such a view is
likely to mean that creative ability is wasted. Many new ideas on
the nature and constitution of creative abilities have been discussed in this book. The overall message for teachers which is
carried in these ideas is that we may have to think in terms of what
I have called 'the ability explosion'. Over recent years we have
become familiar with 'the population explosion', 'the knowledge
explosion', 'the jobs explosion', 'the information explosion', and
many other similar concepts which have been used to describe
the changing patterns of life in the closing decades of the twentieth
century. 'The ability explosion' suggests itself to me as an apt way
of showing the implications for education of some of the new
thinking about the structure of human abilities. The idea of
regarding ability in narrow, purely verbal, formal educational
terms is now no longer tenable. The concept of ability must be
pluralised, and 'abilities' must be the basis of thinking about the
nature of intellect.

This idea of the expanding concept of intelligence is very important for the educator. The structure of intellect model, proposed by Guilford (38) shows clearly that there are 'many different
ways of being intelligent'. The use of different modes of thinking,
using a wide variety of materials, each for a different purpose, can
produce a need for intelligent behaviour which is right outside
that envisaged in formal learning classrooms. Teachers accepting
Guilford's view of intelligence are immediately in the midst of the

ability explosion. The implication is that there are up to a hypothesised 120 different abilities, in Guilford's terms, which may need identifying, providing for, encouraging and guiding. And it is likely that some of these abilities are latent in the majority of children, not just a select few.

I believe that the ability explosion can be seen in the hierarchical structure of intelligence proposed by Vernon (102). Many of the specific abilities at the bottom of his structure (see Figure A) may be regarded as creative and could possibly be represented (as has been done in Figure A) diagrammatically as small *c*'s to denote creative abilities, as distinct from *s*'s to denote specificity only. They would still owe some variance to the abilities higher up the diagram, but nevertheless they would be many in number, creative in their specificity and highly important aspects in planning work with groups of children. Guilford himself has applied similar reasoning to the primary mental abilities suggested by Thurstone.

Figure A

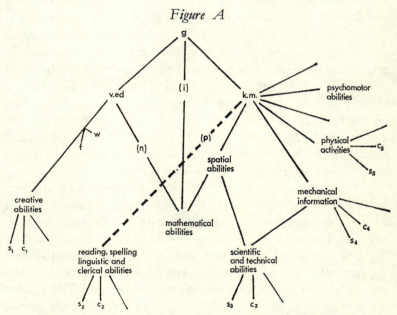

General format of diagram used by Vernon in *Intelligence and Cultural Environment* (Methuen, 1969)

The concept of creativity for the teacher emerges as complex and all-embracing. It is a link which can be shown to connect the philosophical and psychological bases of their work. It can be described as a nexus of education, and so it is a central feature in educational decision-making and the formulation of aims and objectives in schools.

The view of creativity which has been presented in this book is not related to the total pattern of education so much as synonymous with it. Under the canopy of the omnibus title of 'creativity' there exists the what, why and how of education. Decisions regarding what will be taught, for what reasons and the method which will be used are all affected by the concept of creativity, and its place in the educative process, held by the person making the judgement.

Few would quarrel with a speculative look at education in the future which stressed the importance of teaching children to be able to think imaginatively, solve problems using originality, and adapt to changing situations with flexibility. Wolfe (in Downing and Brown (23)) draws particular attention to the need to teach children to think. She suggests that teachers themselves must be competent thinkers if they are to teach others. This is a particularly relevant point which I have applied to creativity in this book on several occasions. Teachers will be better equipped to cater for creative abilities in children if they have extended their own knowledge and awareness of both their own creative potential, and the explanations of its possible origins. There is a feedback from a teacher's own creative endeavours which helps to enrich the efforts of her pupils in their creative activities.

Throughout the book there has been an emphasis on children using originality to solve problems. The original thinker is sure to be at a premium in tomorrow's world. Where so much is automated, where there is so little choice and individual decision to be made, the originator of new ideas will be the innovator, and the innovator will decide subsequent automation. Not everyone will be in this position of manipulation, however. The greater need, in order to avoid a control of people through mass media, is for training in the process of thinking. This, together with the ability to apply originality to thinking, is the means whereby individuals can evaluate and assess decisions taken by others which directly affect them. The last of the ideas postulated in a speculative look at education in the future, is that children should be able to adapt to changing situations with flexibility. How will this be done? I believe that, first, children must have a fund of understanding based on personal experience. Then they need many interests which are capable of absorbing their attention. In Koestler's (55) terms, they need to actualise their surplus potential as distinct from letting it slip away unused. Given these experiences, they require help, especially in the middle years of schooling, with linking first- and second-hand experiences. It is not an easy task to link up one's own experiences with one's reading, the subject-matter introduced by the teacher and the accumulation of knowledge encountered through various forms of mass media. However, it is a task which must be accomplished, and one in which the teacher plays an important part, if pupils are to have the background necessary to adapt with flexibility to changing situations. An insufficient background of knowledge, inadequately understood, will produce stereotyped responses to any stimuli. Flexibility of response and easy adaptation are more likely to come if what is known is thoroughly understood and easily applied and reapplied in new situations. The type of education which will encourage this will be characterised by children following their own interests, deepening their understanding through first-hand inquiry, and being helped to lead off at appropriate tangents, to follow new and perhaps more fruitful lines. The teacher will be available to co-ordinate the studies by assisting pupils to see the connection between the original work and the tangents which led off from it. The links may become difficult to trace and abstract in connection. They will not be seen easily by children. Nevertheless, they are important, as, once they are appreciated, they help the pupil to see the patterns of knowledge, the relationships between different aspects of their studies and the interdependence of most things in their world.

I recall reading an article by Jaquetta Hawkes in which she was discussing her father, Sir Frederick Gowland Hopkins, the distinguished biochemist. She described how he often knew intuitively what the results of his experiments would be, and only went to the bench to confirm his own insight. She attributed this to the fact that he kept his mind fluid, 'a screen of tiny particles of knowledge and experience on which the images of his thought condensed and took shape'. This is the state of mind the educator should encourage as being conducive to both the imaginative posing and creative solving of problems. It is a state invoked by some of the teachers whose work was reported in Chapter 7 and actually illustrated in the responses of the pupils.

In conclusion, I would like to offer a word of caution, and quote Anderson (3), who said: 'Creativity is elusive, intangible, evanescent; as indescribable and indefinable as good health, as intangible and unpredictable as a concept of optimum growth.' My own view is that creativity is like electricity – it is always there, but it needs connecting up and switching on. To continue this analogy, it is worth remembering that sometimes the strongest current often takes some time to build up.

Creativity is the ethos of education today, but it is not the panacea. The teacher who will be successful in applying the principles which have formed the basis for discussion in this book will have two main qualities. Firstly, he will be fully aware of each individual pupil, and realise that each child is a prototype who will never be identically copied. Secondly, he will be deeply concerned about his professional responsibilities, and committed to helping his pupils to realise that aspect of their potential where they feel they have some excellence. I am sure that these two approaches form the basis of successful and satisfying teaching.

SUMMARY

Many of the ideas introduced and discussed in the book are drawn together. They are reviewed generally and more reflectively than in earlier chapters.

The concept of 'an ability explosion' is introduced. This is a term used to convey the idea that it is now no longer tenable to think only of ability in formal educational terms. Rather, the teacher should be concerned with liberating, catering for and extending a wide range, or 'explosion', of abilities, involving both convergent and divergent thinking.

Creativity is presented as a bond in the total educative process, and one of the foundations of pedagogy in the 1970s.

A speculative look is taken at education in the future; and some suggestions regarding the emerging role of the teacher in encouraging creative potential are made.

Appendix 1

ABSTRACT OF THESIS PRESENTED FOR THE DEGREE OF MASTER IN EDUCATION, UNIVERSITY OF MANCHESTER, APRIL 1969

A FACTORIAL STUDY OF CREATIVITY IN JUNIOR SCHOOL CHILDREN

AIM

The investigation attempts to study all aspects of the creative work and thinking of a sample of children in English junior schools. It examines the nature of creativity, the relationship between personality qualities and qualities of creativity and indicates possible means by which creative children may be identified.

THE MEASUREMENT TECHNIQUES

Thirty tests or task situations were administered to the sample. The measures used were of the following type.

1 Intelligence tests (verbal and non-verbal) (5 measures).
2 Achievement tests in English and arithmetic (6 measures).
3 Personality inventories (2 measures).
4 Verbal creativity tests (3 measures).
5 Non-verbal creativity tests (3 measures).
6 Assessment of creative ability in the following areas of the school curriculum (5 measures).

> (a) Physical education.
> (b) Drama.
> (c) Model-making.
> (d) Painting.
> (e) Creative writing.

7 Tests of the creative use of mathematics (2 measures).
8 Assessment of social class (1 measure).
9 Self-ratings, teacher-ratings and peer-ratings of various hypothesised dimensions of creativity (3 measures).

THE SAMPLE

The sample consisted of 265 children, aged 9 to 11 years, drawn from eleven classes in five primary schools. These schools were selected to produce a heterogeneous sample which would cover the range of ability and social class normally found in junior schools.

RESULTS

From the test battery seventy-four variables were extracted. The Atlas computer at Manchester University was used to compute

TABLE 1: *Factor 1. Verbal Intelligence. % variance = 16·522*

Item	Factor loading
Ability and achievement variables:	
N.F.E.R. Primary Verbal 2	0·896
Cornwell Intelligence Test	0·862
General Ability Test (unpublished)	0·894
N.F.E.R. Group Non-Verbal 5	0·817
Ravens Standard Progressive Matrices	0·800
N.F.E.R. Arithmetic Test C.1	0·855
Arithmetic Test C.S. 1965 (unpublished)	0·826
Walmsley Mathematics Test (unpublished)	0·832
N.F.E.R. English Test D.2	0·856
English Test C.S. 1965 (unpublished)	0·833
English Test B. 1962 (unpublished)	0·857
Verbal creativity tests:	
Alternate uses – fluency	0·573
Similarities – fluency	0·492
Ratings of creativity in school activities:	
Creative writing – flexibility	0·413
Creative use of mathematics:	
Creative Maths Test B (unpublished)	0·420
Teacher ratings of creativity:	
Fluency	0·450
Originality	0·440
Flexibility	0·466
Inventiveness	0·404
Elaboration	0·507

intercorrelations. From the resultant matrix a principal components factor analysis was carried out, followed by rotation to a Varimax and to a Promax solution.

In this inquiry the Promax solution resembled very closely the Varimax solution. Analysis of the data was therefore based on the latter. Seventeen factors were extracted from the Varimax analysis, accounting for 71·765 per cent of the total variance. Of these, twelve factors having the greatest variance were analysed, accounting between them for 61·124 per cent of the total variance.

Tables 1 and 2 show the variables in each of the factors detailed having loadings greater than 0·4. Factors are not presented in order as extracted, but grouped for clearer identification.

TABLE 2 : *Personality factors*

Item	Factor loading
Factor 2. General orecticism. % *variance* = 8·264	
C.P.Q. Factor D,　phlegmatic/excitable	0·637
C.P.Q. Factor J,　vigorous/doubting	0·612
C.P.Q. Factor O,　self-assured/apprehensive	0·644
C.P.Q. Factor N,　forthright/shrewd	0·403
C.P.Q. Factor Q4, relaxed/tense	0·673
N.J.M.I. (neuroticism)	0·597
C.P.Q. (2nd order factor), anxiety	0·902
C.P.Q. (3rd order factor), neuroticism	0·777
C.P.Q. Factor A,　reserved/outgoing	− 0·566
C.P.Q. Factor C,　affected by feelings/stable	− 0·583
C.P.Q. Factor G,　disregards rules/conscientious	− 0·464
C.P.Q. Factor H,　shy/venturesome	− 0·749
C.P.Q. Factor Q3, casual/controlled	− 0·438
C.P.Q. (2nd order factor) exvia *v.* invia	− 0·722
Factor 3. Tender-mindedness. % *variance* = 5·278	
C.P.Q. Factor I,　tough-minded/tender-minded	0·810
C.P.Q. Factor G,　disregards rules/conscientous	0·412
C.P.Q. Factor Q3, casual/controlled	0·555
C.P.Q. (3rd order factor), neuroticism	0·560
C.P.Q. Factor D,　phlegmatic/excitable	− 0·444
C.P.Q. Factor E,　obedient/assertive	− 0·787
C.P.Q. Factor F,　sober/happy-go-lucky	− 0·803
C.P.Q. Factor N,　forthright/shrewd	− 0·595

The following factors indicated in Table 3 proved largely specific, i.e. each individual factor contained heavy loadings from one of the areas of creative activity represented in the test battery.

TABLE 3

Factor umber	Factor name	% variance
Creativity factors		
4	Creativity in the plastic arts	3·326
5	Graphical elaboration (circles test)	3·836
6	Creative ability in drama	3·419
7	Creative model-making	3·682
8	Creative ability in physical education	3·786
10	Non-verbal *v.* verbal creativity	2.142
11	Creative writing	3·503
Personal judgement factors		
9	Teacher-rated creativity	4.209
12	Peer opinion	3·157

CONCLUSIONS

There was support for the view that with English primary school children, tests of creativity measure different attributes from those measured in conventional tests of intelligence, and that the two sets of measures have some variance in common which may be attributable to general mental ability, 'g'.

The evidence of this study was against the suggestion that 'creativity, as a dimensional aspect of ability, is a distinct group factor'. There was support for the view that it was highly complex, involving constituent sub-factors which, in this study, revealed themselves as specific content factors.

Although some significant positive relationships were found to exist between high rating in creative school activities and tests of creativity, they occurred in areas which would seem to require similar academic abilities. There was no evidence indicating a factor of creativity influencing both.

There was some suggestion that children showing a high degree of creativity, as measured in this research, tended to be sensitive, tender-minded, conscientious, well-adjusted and somewhat introverted.

There was a statistically significant relationship at the 1 per cent level (correlations ranged from 0·2 to 0·5) between creative ability and attainment in English and arithmetic, but this only occurred where verbal attributes were present on the creativity side.

Teacher judgements of creativity were found to be biased towards academic attainment and, along with peer nominations of creativity, showed low correlations with results of creativity tests.

Self-rating of creativity, using questionnaire techniques, was found to be a poor indicator of creative ability as measured by tests.

There was no evidence in this study that creativity in school was related to the social class of the parents of the children in the sample.

Appendix 2

SUGGESTED PROCEDURES FOR RANKING THE CHILDREN IN THE SAMPLE

All rating must be carried out according to the criteria set out in the schedules prepared for each activity.

RANKING IN ART, CREATIVE WRITING AND MODEL-MAKING

As these activities involve rating a product, the following procedure is suggested:

1. Pick out the best five products.
2. Pick out the worst five products.
3. Pick out the five products which are next to the best.
4. Pick out the five products which are next to the worst.
5. Assess the remaining products picking out the next five best, then the next five worst and so on . . . until all the products have been initially grouped.
6. Take the best group and place them in order of merit for the variable under consideration.
7. Take the next best group and continue with the ranking.
8. Continue all through the groups.

RANKING IN PHYSICAL EDUCATION

As this activity involves rating performances, the following procedure is suggested:

1. As each child is seen carrying out an activity, assign a numerical grade on a 5-point scale for each of the variables under consideration (i.e. fluency, flexibility, originality).

2   Add the fluency scores for each situation rated to achieve a composite score for 'fluency'.

3   Repeat this for the flexibility and originality scores.

4   Use these totals to arrange pupils in rank order, but check that the position of each child corresponds to your overall impression. Reconsider and amend until you are satisfied with your order of merit.

RANKING IN DRAMA

Rating here involves assessing a performance and the suggestions for ranking performance in physical education should be followed, with the exception that, as there is only one performance in drama, no 'summing' of scores to achieve a composite score will be necessary.

Bibliography

1. Anastasi, A. *Psychological Testing* (Macmillan, 2nd ed., 1966 impression)

2. Anderson, H. H. (Ed.). *Creativity and Its Cultivation* (Harper and Brothers, New York 1959)

3. Anderson, H. H. (Ed.). *Creativity in Childhood and Adolescence. A Diversity of Approach* (Palo Alto, Calif., Science and Behaviour Books Inc. 1965)

4. Barron, F. *Creativity and Psychological Health* (Princeton, N.J., Van Nostrand 1963)

5. Barron, F. 'The Disposition towards Originality' (pp. 139–52) in Taylor, C. W. and Barron, F. (Eds.), *Scientific Creativity. Its Recognition and Development* (New York, John Wiley & Sons 1964)

6. Bloom, B. S. (Ed.). *Taxonomy of Educational Objectives: the Classification of Educational Goals*, Handbook 1, The Cognitive Domain (McKay & Co. 1956)

7. Bloom, R. S. 'Testing Cognitive Ability and Achievement' in *Handbook of Research on Teaching*. M. L. Gage (Chicago, Rand McNally 1963)

7a. Bohm, D. *On Creativity*, Leonardo, Vol. 1, 137–49 (Pergamon Press 1968)

8. Bridges, S. A. *Gifted Children and the Brentwood Experiment* (Pitman 1969)

9. Bruner, J. S. 'The Conditions of Creativity' in Gruber, H. E. Terrell, G. & Wertheimer, M. (Eds.), *Contemporary Approaches to Creative Thinking* (New York, Atherton Press 1962)

10. Burt, C. 'The Structure of the Mind', *Brit. J. Educ. Psychol.*, 19, 180 f. (1949)

11. Burt, C. 'The Psychology of Creative Ability' (critical notice of Getzels, J. W. and Jackson, P. W., *Creativity and Intelligence*, London and New York, John Wiley), *Brit. J. Educ. Psychol.*, November 1962, 32, 3, 292

12. Burt, C. Foreword in *The Act of Creation*, Koestler, A. (Hutchinson, London 1964)

13. Burt, C. 'Factorial Studies of Personality and Their Bearing on the Work of the Teacher', *Brit. J. Educ. Psychol.*, **35,** 368–78 (1965)

14. Charles, D. C. *Psychology of the Child in the Classroom* (New York, Macmillan 1964)

15. Cheong, G. J. C. 'Relations among Experimental Attitudes, Creativity, School Attitude and Sociometric Status of Fourth–sixth-grade Pupils', *The Journal of Teacher Education*, **18,** 2 (Summer 1967)

16. Cropley, A. J. 'Originality, Intelligence and Personality', unpublished doctoral thesis, University of Alberta, reported in the *Australian Journal of Education*, **2,** 2, 120–5 (June 1967)

17. Cropley, A. J. 'Creativity and Intelligence', *Brit. J. Educ. Psychol.*, **36,** 259–66 (1966)

18. Cropley, A. J. *Creativity* (Longmans 1967)

19. Cropley, A. J. 'A Note on the Wallach-Kogan Tests of Creativity', *Brit. J. Educ. Psychol.*, **38,** 2, 197–201 (June 1968)

20. Cross, P. G., Cattell, R. B. & Butcher, H. J. 'The Personality Patterns of Creative Artists', *Brit. J. Educ. Psychol.*, **37,** 3, 292–9 (November 1967)

21. Davies, E. C. & Miller, D. M. *The Philosophic Process in Physical Education* (Lea and Febbinger 1967)

22. Dearden, R. F. *The Philosophy of Primary Education* (Routledge and Kegan Paul 1968)

23. Downing, J. & Brown. *The Third International Reading Symposium*, article by J. B. Wolfe (Cassell 1968)

24. Drevdahl, J. E. 'Some Developmental and Environmental Factors in Creativity', pp. 170–86 in Taylor, C. W. (Ed.), *Widening Horizons in Creativity* (New York, Wiley 1964)

25. Edwards, E. P. & Tyler, L. E. 'Intelligence, Creativity and Achievement in a Non-selective Public Junior High School', *Journal of Educational Psychology*, **56,** 96–9 (1965)

26. Eysenck, H. J. *The Structure of Human Personality* (London, Methuen 1960)

27. Fleming, C. M. *Teaching. A Psychological Analysis* (Methuen 1958)

28. Freeman, J., Butcher H. J. & Christie, T. *Creativity. A Selective Review of Research* (Society for Research into Higher Education 1968)

29. Fromm, E. 'The Creative Attitude', in Anderson, H. H. (2, *op. cit.*) (1959)

30. Gardner, S. F. 'Creativity in Children. A Study of the Relationship between Temperamental Factors and Aptitude Factors involved in the Creative Ability of Seventh Grade Children, with Suggestions for a Theory of Creativity', *Dissertation Abstracts*, **24,** 822 (1964)

31. Garnett, J. C. M. 'General Ability, Cleverness and Purpose', *Brit. J. Educ. Psychol.*, **9** (1919)

32. Getzels, J. W. & Jackson, P. W. *Creativity and Intelligence* (London and New York, John Wiley & Sons, Inc. 1962)

33. Ghiselin, B. (Ed.). *The Creative Process. A Symposium* (New York, Mentor 1955)

34. Goldman, R. J. 'The Minnesota Tests of Creative Thinking', *Educational Research* **7**, 1, 3 (1964)

35. Goldman, R. J. & Clarke, D. F. 'The Minnesota Tests of Creative Thinking: A Note on Scorer Reliability in Follow-up Studies with English Primary School Children', *Brit. J. Educ. Psychol.*, **37**, 1, 115–17 (February 1967)

36. Gowan, J. C. *Annotated Bibliography on Creativity and Giftedness* (San Fernando Valley State College Foundation, Northridge, California 1965)

37. Grobman, H. *Evaluation Activities of Curriculum Projects. A Starting Point* (Rand McNally 1968)

38. Guilford, J. P. 'Three Faces of Intellect', *Amer. Psychologist*, **14**, 469–79 (1959)

39. Guilford, J. P. 'Traits of Creativity', in Anderson, H. H. (Ed.), *Creativity and Its Cultivation* 31–9 (New York, Harper 1959)

40. Guilford, J. P. 'A Psychometric Approach to Creativity', in Anderson, H. H. (Ed.), *Creativity in Childhood and Adolescence* (Science and Behaviour Books Inc. 1965)

41. Guilford, J. P. *The Nature of Human Intelligence* (McGraw-Hill 1967)

42. Guilford, J. P. & others. 'Creative Thinking in Children at the Junior High School Level' (Los Angeles, University of Southern California, Psychological Laboratory, Report No. 26 1961) (Mimeo)

43. Haefele, J. W. *Creativity and Innovation* (Reinhold Management Reference Series, Reinhold Pub. Corp. 1962)

44. Hargreaves, H. L. 'The Faulty of Imagination', *Brit. J. Educ. Psychol.*, Monograph Supplement X (1927)

45. Hart, A. 'A Study of Creative Thinking and Its Relation to Nursing', unpublished Ed.D. thesis (Bloomington, Indiana University, 1962), in *Dissertation Abstracts*, **23**, 4, 323 (1963)

46. Hasan, P. & Butcher, H. J. 'Creativity and Intelligence: A Partial Replication with Scottish Children of Getzels and Jackson's Study', *Brit. J. Educ. Psychol.*, **57**, 1 & 2, 129–35 (1966)

47. Hildreth, G. H. *Introduction to the Gifted* (New York, McGraw Hill 1966)

48. Holland, J. L. 'Some Limitations of Teacher Ratings as Predictors of Creativity', *Journal of Educational Psychology*, **50**, 219–23 (1959)

49. Hudson, L. 'Contrary Imaginations (London, Methuen 1966)

50. Hughes, H. K. 'The Enhancement of Creativity', *Journal of Creative Behaviour*, **3**, 2 (Spring 1969)

M

51. Hughes, P. W. 'Changes in Primary Curriculum in Tasmania', *The Australian Journal of Education*, **13**, 2, 130–47 (June 1969)

52. James, C. *Young Lives at Stake* (Collins 1968)

53. Kelley, T. L. 'The Boundaries of the Mental Life', excerpts from *Crossroads in the Mind of Man* (1928) Stanford University Press, appearing in Wiseman, S., *Intelligence and Ability* (London, Penguin 1967)

54. Kneller, G. F. *The Art and Science of Creativity* (Holt, Reinhart and Winston 1967)

55. Koestler, A. *The Act of Creation* (London, Hutchinson 1964)

56. Lait, M. R. 'The Relationship of Various School Factors to Creativity', unpublished doctoral dissertation at San Fernando Valley State College, California (1964)

57. Lawton, D. *Social Class, Language and Education* (Routledge and Kegan Paul 1968)

58. Lovell, K. *Team Teaching* (University of Leeds Institute of Education, Paper No. 5 1967)

59. Lovell, K. & Shields, J. B. 'Some Aspects of the Study of the Gifted Child', *Brit. J. Educ. Psychol.*, **37**, 2 (June 1967)

60. MacDonald, J. *A Philosophy of Education* (Scott, Foresman & Co. 1965)

61. MacKinnon, D. W. 'Personality Correlates of Creativity', a paper presented at the second conference on thinking (National Education Association, Washington, D.C. 2–4 May 1963 (Mimeo)

62. Mackworth, N. H. 'Originality', *American Psychologist* **20** (1965)

63. Marsh, R. W. 'A Statistical Re-analysis of Getzels and Jackson's Data', research note in *Brit. J. Educ. Psychol.*, **34**, 91–3 (1964)

64. Maslow, A. H. 'Creativity in Self-actualising People', in Anderson, H. H. (Ed.), *Creativity and Its Cultivation* (Harper & Row 1959)

65. May, F. B. 'Creative Thinking: A Factorial Study of Seventh-grade Children', unpublished Ph.D. thesis, Madison University of Wisconsin, 1961, in *Dissertation Abstracts*, **22**, 1876–1961

66. McGuire, C. *Personality Correlates of Creativity*, Report No. 13 (Austin, University of Texas, Laboratory of Human Behaviour, Department of Educational Psychology (1963). Reported by Gowan (1965)

67. McIntyre, D., Morrison, A. & Sutherland, J. 'Social and Educational Variables relating to Teachers' Assessments of Primary School Pupils', *Brit. J. Educ. Psychol.*, **36**, 3, 272–9 (November 1966)

68. McKellar, P. *Imagination and Thinking* (London, Cohen & West 1957)

69. McNemar, Q. 'Lost: Our Intelligence. Why?', *Amer. Psychologist*, **19**, 871–82 (1964)

70. Mednick, S. A. 'The Association Concept of the Creative Process', *Psychological Review*, **69,** 220–32 (1962)

71. Nelson, H. F. 'Creativity – Its Psychological Implications.' Paper read at the American Industrial Arts Association, Twenty-fourth Annual Convention, Pittsburg, Pennsylvania, 18 April 1962

72. Nuss, E. M. 'An Exploration of the Relationship between Creativity and Certain Personal-social Variables among 8th grade pupils', unpublished Ed.D. thesis, College Park, University of Maryland, 1961, *Dissertation Abstracts*, **22,** 3,045 (1962)

73. Parker, D. H. *Schooling for Individual Excellence* (London, Nelson 1963)

74. Pribram, K. H. 'Neurological Notes on the Art of Educating', in Hilgard, E. R. (Ed.), *N.S.S.E. Year Book, 1963* (Chicago, University of Chicago Press)

75. Reid, L. A. *Philosophy and Education* (Heinemann 1962)

76. Richards, J. M., Cline, V. B. & Needham, W. E. 'Creativity Tests and Teacher- and Self-judgements of Originality'. *Journal of Experimental Education*, **32,** 3 (Spring 1964)

77. Richmond, W. K. *The Teaching Revolution* (Methuen 1967)

78. Ripple, R. E. & May, F. B. 'Caution in Comparing Creativity and I.Q.', in Ripple, R. E., *Readings in Learning and Human Abilities.* (New York, Harper & Row 1964)

79. Rivlen, L. G. 'Creativity and the Self-attitude and Sociability of High School Students', *Journal of Educational Psychology*, 50, 147–152, (August 1959)

80. Rogers, C. R. *On Becoming a Person* (Constable 1961)

81. Rogers, C. R. 'Towards a Theory of Creativity', pp. 64–72 in Parnes, S. V. & Harding, H. F. (Eds.), *A Source Book for Creative Thinking* (New York, Charles Scribner & Sons 1962)

82. Rosenthal, R. & Jacobson, L. *Pygmalion in the Classroom* (Holt, Reinhart & Winston 1968)

83. Schachtel, E. G. 'Metamorphosis: On the Development of Affect, Perception, Attention and Memory', in Getzels & Jackson (New York, Basic Books 1962)

84. Smith, F. V. Critical notice of Hudson, L., *Contrary Imaginations* (London, Methuen 1966), in *Brit. J. Educ. Psychol.*, **36,** 3, 334–5 (November 1966)

85. Stein, M. K. *Survey of the Psychological Literature in the Area of Creativity, with a View towards Needed Research*, Co-operative Research project No. E–3 (Research Center for Human Relations, New York University 1962)

86. Sultan, E. E. 'A Factorial Study in the Domain of Creative Thinking', *Brit. J. Educ. Psychol.*, **32,** 78–82 (1962)

87. Tagiuri. 'Movement as a Cue in Person Perception', in David, H. P. & Brengelmann (Eds.), *Perspectives in Personality Research* (Springer 1960)

88. Taylor, C. W. (Ed.). *Creativity: Progress and Potential* (New York, McGraw Hill 1964)

89. Taylor, C. W. & Barron, F. *Scientific Creativity: Its Recognition and Development* (2nd printing) (New York, John Wiley & Sons Ltd. 1964)

90. Taylor, C. W. & Williams, F. E. (Eds.). *Instructional Media and Creativity* (Wiley 1966)

91. Thorndike, R. L. 'Some Methodological Issues in the Study of Creativity', in Gardner, S. F., *Proceedings of the 1962 Invitational Conference on Testing Problems* (Princeton, N. J., Educational Testing Service 1963)

92. Thurstone, L. L. 'Creative Talent', in Thurstone, L. L. (Ed.), *Application of Psychology* (New York, Harper 1952)

93. Torrance, E. P. *Guiding Creative Talent* (Englewood Cliffs, N. J., Prentice-Hall Inc. 1962)

94. Torrance, E. P. *Creativity and Intelligence* (Minnesota Bureau of Educational Research, Spring 1963)

95. Torrance, E. P. 'Exploration in Creative Thinking in the Early School Years. A Progress Report', (pp. 173–83) in Taylor, C. W. & Barron, F. (Eds.), *Scientific Creativity: Its Recognition and Development*, 2nd ed. (New York, John Wiley & Sons 1964)

96. Torrance, E. P. *Rewarding Creative Behaviour. Experiments in Classroom Creativity* (Englewood Cliffs, N. J., Prentice-Hall, Inc. 1965)

97. Torrance, E. P. 'Creativity' *New Education*, 6–9 (London, May 1965)

98. Torrance, E. P. & Gowan, J. C. *The Reliability of the Minnesota Tests of Creative Thinking* (Minneapolis University of Minnesota Bureau of Educational Research August 1963)

99. Vernon, P. E. *The Structure of Human Abilities* (London, Methuen 1950)

100. Vernon, P. E. 'The Classification of Abilities', *Educational Research*, **2,** 3 (June 1960)

101. Vernon, P. E. 'Creativity and Intelligence', *Educational Research*, **6,** 3, p. 1,963 (1964)

102. Vernon, P. E. *Intelligence and Cultural Environment* (Methuen 1969)

103. Vinacke. *The Psychology of Thinking* (McGraw Hill 1952)

104. Wall, W. D. 'Highly Intelligent Children. Part 1, The Psychology of the Gifted', *Educational Research*, **2,** 2 (1960)

105. Wall, W. B. 'Highly Intelligent Children. Part 2, The Education of the Gifted', *Educational Research*, **2,** 3 (June 1960)

106. Wallach, M. A. & Kogan, N. *Modes of Thinking in Young Children* (Holt, Reinhart & Winston 1965)

107. Wallen, N. E. 'Creativity – Fantasy and Fact', *Education Digest*, **30**, 1, 18–20 (September 1964)

108. Ward, J. W. 'An Oblique Factorisation of Wallach and Kogan's "Creativity" Correlations', *Brit. J. Educ. Psychol.*, **37**, 3 (November 1967)

109. Wertheimer, M. *Productive Thinking* (Tavistock Publications 1961)

110. Williams, F. E. 'Teacher Competency in Creativity', *Education Today*, July/August 1968, 7–12.

111. Wodtke, K. H. 'Some Data on the Reliability and Validity of Creativity Tests at the Elementary School Level', *Educational and Psychological Measurement*, **24**, 2, 339–408 (1964)

112. Wonderley, D. M. 'A Study of Creative Females', *Gifted Child Quarterly*, **8**, 38–9 (Spring 1964)

113. Yamamoto, K. *Experimental Scoring Manuals for Minnesota Tests of Creative Thinking and Writing* (Kent, Ohio, Bureau of Educational Research, Kent State University 1964)

114. Yamamoto, K. 'Evaluation of Some Creativity Measures in a High School with Peer Nominations as Criteria', *Journal of Psychology*, **58**, 215–93 (1964)

115. Yamamoto, K. 'Role of Creative Thinking and Intelligence in High School Achievement', *Psychological Reports*, **14**, 783–9 (1964)

116. Yamamoto, K. 'Effects of Restriction of Range and Test Unreliability on Correlation between Measures of Intelligence and Creative Thinking', *Brit. J. Educ. Psychol.*, **35**, 300–5 (November 1965)

Glossary

APPREHENSION. One of the dimensions of personality suggested by Cattell. (See Cattell, R. B. *The Scientific Analysis of Personality*, Pelican, 1965.)

AUTISTIC THINKING. ('A' Thinking.) A term used extensively by McKellar (see Bibliography, reference 68), who defines it as 'thinking which is dominated by processes of the fantasy kind rather than geared to reality, e.g. hallucination'. (Contrast this with 'R' Thinking.)

CONSCIENTIOUSNESS. One of the dimensions of personality suggested by Cattell (see reference under APPREHENSION). Persons showing this quality are likely to be strict observers of rules, somewhat conformist and conscientious in doing what is asked of them.

CONVERGENT THINKING. A kind of thinking characterised by its dependence on reproduction of something learned previously, and of using old responses in new situations in a more or less mechanical way. It is suggested that convergent thinking is required to answer questions in normal verbal reasoning tests where only one correct answer is acceptable. Compare this with DIVERGENT THINKING.

CONVERGER. A term used by Hudson (see Bibliography reference 49) who says: 'The converger is the boy who is substantially better at the intelligence test than he is at the open-ended tests.' Compare this with the DIVERGER.

CORRELATION. Correlation is concerned with the correspondence of any two sets of measurements for a group of people.

CORRELATION COEFFICIENT. This is an index for expressing the correspondence between any two sets of measurements for a group of people. If all the children in the sample scored exactly the same score on both tests, it would imply perfect correlation. This would be expressed as $+1\cdot0$. The index ranges from this, through $0\cdot0$ (no agreement either way) to $-1\cdot0$ (negative or inverse agreement). See Dr King's book in the Further Reading section of Chapter 1 for more detailed information.

CREATIVITY TESTS. These are usually open-ended tests, i.e. there are many answers which are possible, all of which would be considered correct. They are contrasted with the normal objective test where there is only one correct answer – i.e. verbal reasoning tests – and tests of achievement in arithmetic and English. Examples of creativity tests are given in Chapter 4.

CRITERIA. The plural of criterion, which in this context refers to a principle, standard or some other measure against which a test is judged. For example, if a test is devised to pick out athletic prowess, its VALIDITY could be measured by its ability to pick out boys who have a history of success in school athletics. Thus the criterion is the thing we are trying to predict. In a subject where many tests already exist, these can be used as criteria to assess the validity of a new test which is being constructed.

DIVERGENT THINKING. A kind of thinking which involves chiefly the production of many and varied responses rather than finding of single correct solutions. It involves fluency, flexibility and originality of response, and is probably similar to what Bartlett calls 'open thinking'. Contrast with CONVERGENT THINKING.

DIVERGER. A term used by Hudson (see Bibliography, reference 49). The diverger is a boy who is substantially better on open-ended or creativity-type tests than he is at intelligence tests. Hudson points out that many people are all-rounders: they have relative fluency in both kinds of tests without there being any substantial difference in their performance on one when compared with the other. Compare this with the CONVERGER.

EXTRAVERSION. One of the dimensions of personality particularly associated with the work of Eysenck. Persons who are considered more extravert have interests which are directed outwards to nature and other people. Contrast with INTROVERSION.

EXTRAVERT. A person who exhibits qualities of EXTRAVERSION.

HALO EFFECT. This is a tendency to be biased in an estimation or rating of an individual by some quite irrelevant impression of the same individual. For example, a teacher receiving a child for the first time may be biased towards the child from having heard comments (either good or bad) from colleagues. Halo effect is a frequent source of error in employing rating scales.

INDICES OF DISCRIMINATION. If a test is used to select certain people and reject others, we need to know whether individual items are doing a good job. The index of discrimination is a device which helps to assess these items. Items with a discrimination index of + 0·3 or above are considered to have good predictive value. There are reasons for including items with an index of less than + 0·3 – for example, to ease a child into the test. For a fuller explanation see Crocker, A. C., *Statistics for the Teacher* (Penguin Education 1969).

INDIVIDUAL COGNITIVE STYLE. This is a phrase used by some psychologists to indicate a particular approach to learning and problem-solving adopted by an individual. For example, one person may learn easily by listening to the spoken word, while another may learn best by studying diagrams. Given the same mathematical problem, one person may solve it best by constructing a model, while another person could do it most easily using algebraic symbols. Each of these people have their own 'individual cognitive style'.

INTER-RATER COMPATIBILITY. A knowledge of CORRELATION and the CORRELATION COEFFICIENT is essential to the understanding of inter-rater compatibility. If two people rate an action or a product, there is a likelihood of a broad measure of agreement if both are adhering to the instructions given and both have expert knowledge of the subject. Inter-rater compatibility is concerned with measuring the degree to which the two raters agree, using a correlation coefficient. Interpretation of the various inter-rater compatibilities is given in the text.

INTROVERSION. One of the dimensions of personality particularly associated with the work of Eysenck. Persons who are considered more introvert have interests which are directed inwards to the thoughts and feelings of the self. Contrast with EXTRAVERSION.

INTROVERT. A person who exhibits qualities of INTROVERSION.

NEUROTICISM. One of the dimensions of personality particularly associated with the work of Eysenck. A term which has many vague, general meanings in everyday speech. Caution is urged in its indiscriminate use. A person exhibiting qualities of neuroticism lacks the stability associated with normal functioning. Interested readers should consult Eysenck, H. J., *The Structure of Human Personality* (Methuen 1960).

PEER NOMINATIONS OF CREATIVITY. Pupils are asked to nominate their friends who best fit certain requirements, e.g. 'Who in your class has the most wild and silly ideas?' It is suggested that these nominations by peers can assist in helping teachers to identify creative children, but the evidence for this is very tenuous.

PRIMARY TRAITS OF CREATIVITY. It has been suggested by Guilford (see Bibliography, reference 39) that attributes such as FLUENCY in the production of ideas, FLEXIBILITY of thinking, ORIGINALITY of response, and the ability to INVENT and ELABORATE on simple stimuli are characteristics which identify 'high creatives'. Conflicting evidence has been produced regarding this (see Chapter 1), but the idea is productive for the teacher, as is shown throughout this book.

PRODUCTIVE THINKING. A term now usually associated with Wertheimer (see Bibliography, reference 109), who uses it to describe thinking which is born of an inherent curiosity. It is suggested that this style of thinking occurs because men long for it. Wertheimer is concerned to analyse it, document it, and provide a means of improving it. The term was also used last century by Galton, who called it 'a higher mental process', and tried to devise tests to measure it.

PSYCHOMETRICS. This is one of the academic disciplines associated with the study of education. It is concerned with the measurement of behaviour, and is characterised by a statistical approach.

REALITY THINKING. ('R' Thinking.) A term used extensively by McKellar (see Bibliography, reference 68), who defines it as 'thinking constrained by concern with observable facts, and characterised by connection of a logical (rather than merely associative) kind, e.g. scientific thinking and logical reasoning'. (Contrast this with 'A' THINKING.)

RELIABILITY. The reliability of a test is concerned with the extent to which it gives similar results if it is repeated. It is reliable if the results, when the test is given on separate occasions, are similar. Thus reliability is a measure of the consistency of the test, and can be assessed by several methods:

1. TEST RE-TEST: where the same test is given twice, with a gap of about a month between the administrations. The scores on each test are compared by a CORRELATION technique, and an index of reliability or reliability coefficient is computed.
2. PARALLEL FORMS: two similar versions of a test are given and the results compared.
3. SPLIT HALF: In this method the odd-numbered items in the tests are correlated with the even-numbered items.

Most elementary textbooks of educational statistics discuss both reliability and validity of tests in detail.

SENSITIVITY. A term used to describe an aspect of personality in this book. Persons having this quality of sensitivity are very receptive to stimuli and governed more by the emotions than realistic, logical thinking.

SOCIAL CLASS. Many studies classify individuals according to social class. This is usually done by ascertaining the employment of the person (or the parent in the case of a school study). The researcher then looks up the occupation in the Registrar-General's Classification of Occupations to see which of the five prestige groupings it has been placed in. It sometimes denotes all those individuals (or families) who possess, within the framework of some society or community, relatively the same amounts of power, income, wealth or prestige.

TENDER-MINDEDNESS. One of the dimensions of personality used by Cattell (see reference under APPREHENSION), but first suggested by William James in the early 1900s. Persons exhibiting this quality are intuitive, governed by sentiment, sensitive to the feelings of others and sympathetic.

VALIDITY. The validity of a test is concerned with the degree to which it measures what it purports to measure. It is customary to consider a test valid if a high correlation is found between the test and a satisfactory independent criterion. The psychologist assesses several kinds of validity:

1. FACE VALIDITY, which is established by considering the degree to which the test seems on face value to measure what it purports to measure. A page of sums would appear to the layman to measure arithmetical ability.

2. PREDICTIVE VALIDITY, which is the ability of the test to predict some future result. For example, an eleven plus test could be considered as a predictor of academic performance at sixteen and eighteen plus. The degree to which it was successful would be a measure of its predictive validity.

3. CONSTRUCT VALIDITY, which is assessed by analysing the test to try to demonstrate the presence of a quality or construct which the test is trying to measure.

4. CONCURRENT VALIDITY, which is an attempt to show validity by estimating something we cannot measure directly. For example, we watch the mercury in a thermometer and infer the temperature from that. It is sometimes assessed by correlating test scores with the ratings of experienced judges, gathered at about the same time, on the skill being assessed.

5. CONTENT VALIDITY which involves a logical analysis of the content of the test, and a comparison of this with subject-matter, content, and behaviour which might have been included. Thus, if a test contains important aspects of the course, i.e. it matches what the teacher has been trying to teach, it could have a high content validity.

Most elementary textbooks of educational statistics deal with the validity of tests in some detail.

Index